ANCIENT BLOODED HEALER

You're One Of A Kind

HANNAH ANDREWS
Reality Awareness: *Awakening the Consciousness of Humanity*

Reality Awareness: *Awakening the Consciousness of Humanity*

Copyright © 2023
REALITY AWARENESS
HANNAH ANDREWS
ANCIENT BLOODED HEALER
You're One Of A Kind
All rights reserved.

No part of this publication may be reproduced, distributed, or transmitted in any form or by any means, including photocopying, recording, or other electronic or mechanical methods, without the prior written permission of the publisher, except in the case of brief quotations embodied in critical reviews and certain other non-commercial uses permitted by copyright law.

REALITY AWARENESS
HANNAH ANDREWS

Printed Worldwide
First Printing 2023
First Edition 2023

ISBN: 978-0-6458512-0-5 (paperback)
ISBN: 978-0-6458512-1-2 (kindle book)
ISBN: 978-0-6458512-2-9 (epub ebook)

Disclaimer:

The information in this book is intended for educational and entertainment purposes only. Any names or identifying traits of stories or results shared, have been changed to protect their identities or have been used with permissions. Any resemblance to actual persons, living or dead, or actual events is purely coincidental.

Any information contained in this book does not at any time replace the services and advice of qualified professionals in the medical and mental health fields, other health care professionals, practitioners of any kind or legal advice. It is recommended to seek service providers in their own field of expertise where required. Please note that by reading and/or using this information, audios and other means of services and products provided and recommended by the author and Reality Awareness in this book, you do so at your own risk.

This book and material at Reality Awareness may use some psychodynamic processes that rely on uncovering unconsciousness material to promote change. With this, you take full responsibility for participating in the activities within your safe limits. The Author, Publisher and Reality Awareness, our facilitators, employees, agents, contractors or consultants accept no responsibility whatsoever for any injury, illness, death, loss, economic hardship or other outcome that may result during or after from your actions

To all my dear clients who allow me to hold deep space for them, for all those who have walked a hard past alone in the dark,
I see you.
To all those who crossed my path to shine light on a darkness I never knew existed, to transform darkness to light, it is here we walk forward,
Awakening the Consciousness of Humanity.
Together, intricately woven through the fabric of life, without you, this book wouldn't be here.
This, is for you.

Table of Contents

Ancient Blooded Healer   1
You're One of a Kind

Chapter 2   13
The Makings of An Ancient Blooded Healer

Chapter 3   71
The Subconscious Is So Clear To You

Chapter 4   91
Wisdom Walkers

Chapter 5   125
Your Values Activate Your Life Purpose

Chapter 6   137
Understanding Your Ancient Blooded Healer Gifts

Chapter 7   169
Different Fears That Halt Your Life Purpose

Chapter 8   203
Stepping Out Into the World As An Ancient Blooded Healer

Chapter 9   213
Final Words

Ancient Blooded Healer

You're One Of A Kind

I was on the beach, my favourite place and healing space. I was sitting there, crying. I was so upset and devastated because I couldn't understand why he would lie to me like that. I was pouring my heart out to the Angels, Archangels, Mermaids, God, and whoever would listen when I felt this shiver all over my body. And then I saw it. Like a line down the centre of my arms, all these thin white feathers lifted out of my arms. I opened my eyes, stretching to see through my tear-filled eyes. 'This is what you can feel,' I heard.

My breath shook with the sobs from my crying as I was shown how sensitive I was. I rubbed my hand down my arm to make sure I was seeing what I was seeing, and they 'flattened'. I was being shown how sensitive *you* are. How sensitive we are. How sensitive Ancient Blooded Healers are.

He was telling the truth. I was picking up something completely different—something they were not even aware of. No wonder I seemed like a crazy person again. He had gone to a party without me again. I thought he was cheating on me because I could feel a shift in the atmosphere around me at home. I saw the connection between them. And I was right. And yet, he was only talking to her, and she to him. But there was a vibe between them, a deeper connection, and *that* is what I felt. That is what sent me into a spin. But that is 'all it was'—the deeper connection I felt underneath.

The feathers on my arms showed me how sensitively I pick up vibrations, even from miles away. Just like animals pick up the slightest change in the atmospheric energy or vibrational earth patterns, so do we, the Ancient Blooded Healers, have the same deep intuitive sense.

It took me a while to realise this. I just thought everyone could and does pick up this level of subtle vibrations and that this is normal. But it is not normal.

Not to people who are not Ancient Blooded Healers. To us, it is normal. Most times, we don't even realise we are doing it or sensing it, so we either ignore it, brush it off, or have learnt to shut it out because being called crazy and fucked up in the head by the ones you love, well, that's not a nice feeling. So we shut down instead.

I was having a lunch catch-up with two of my besties in October 2017, and one shared how her mother had just been diagnosed with stomach cancer. The other was speaking about all these healing techniques and where they were coming from, and I was listening as I was eating but shaking my head. 'No,' I butted in and proceeded to share the vision of the diagnosis I was receiving about where it came from, which generational lineage it came from, what age she was when the trauma originally happened, and what she needed to look at metaphysically for it to heal. They both had stopped eating and were staring at me when I realised I had just butted in and shared all that. With teary eyes looking at me, she said, 'Yes, I will definitely pass that onto her.' And she confirmed what I had said, as her mother had shared some of that information with her recently, and then they were like, 'How did you know that?' I was shocked. 'Um, what do you mean? Didn't you both see that and know that too?' 'No, Hannah, you have a gift.' 'What? Isn't this normal?' I was stunned. Oh.

I knew I was gifted, psychic, talented, and on point with my intuition, psychic readings, intuitive healings, and the like. By that stage, I had been in this career for 12 years, since my spiritual awakening when I was 21 in 2005. But that moment in time, at that table with my two besties, has been etched into my memory like it was yesterday.

Something changed in me that day. It made me more humble at the same time that 100 million experiences flashed back through my mind as I drove home, almost bringing me to tears in realising why everyone would look at me weird when I am 'just speaking normally' or the number of times I had been called crazy, dumb, stupid, ridiculous, fucked up in the head, or lose groups of friends very fast no matter how many different groups I would try to make friends in when I am just being myself and talking... well, what I thought was normal.

It was here that I realised just how deep my gift went. I started to look at myself differently. I started to see myself. I started to understand my life, why everything up to this moment in time had happened the way it did, and why I never felt understood. After all, I was just talking normally; isn't this normal for everyone?

No, honey.

We are

Ancient Blooded Healers

And we are

One Of A Kind.

During that on-and-off relationship, he kept pointing the finger at me, saying it was all my fault; everything that went wrong in our relationship was my fault, that I was the cause of it all, and that MY reactions were the issue. At 30 years old, I took it to heart and looked deep within myself. This was the start of many counselling sessions with a psychologist, healer, and deeply connected being for whom I am ever so grateful. I had many sessions with her for years because of what he said, trying to 'figure out what was wrong with me'.

My deepest realisation of the Ancient Blooded Healer lineage came like a dawning light that changed EVERYTHING for me in the blink of an eye in one of the sessions with her. She looked me in the eye and said,

'Like, you're a different species.'

Time stood still as those words poured out of her mouth in slow motion. And all of a sudden, EVERYTHING on this planet made sense. All the missing pieces of the puzzle of my life came together and made complete sense.

Ancient Blooded Healer

Welcome Home.

This book is a reference guide for you to come back to time and time again. It is a reference for when you feel like everyone has turned their back on you. It is a space to return to when you forget who you are because you're so different from everyone else that you question everything you do frequently, especially when you find the thing that lights you up again!

Ancient Blooded Healers feel more than anyone. Some people label this as 'Empaths'. But we are something else. It is deeper than Empath.

You have walked this earth since the dawning of time. Your lineage belongs here. Not the stars, not the planets, but here.

You are a crystalline lineage. Being that you began on this earth, on this realm, you have inside of you something that connects you deeper to this realm than anyone else who walks these lands. This is your gift, your point of difference, and your lineage. You're definitely...

One Of A Kind.

We are a different breed.

I would always screw my face up at others when they would talk about their star home and how clear their connection was to feel like their home was not here on earth when their Galactic Being was their brother and that they could speak to them about the galactic federation past Andromeda and the gobbly goop 7th dimension constellation that is coming in on the 28th of

November at 7:17 a.m. past this galaxy drive. They are Starseed Lumerian Guide Gorgarians from Sirius B and talk to Pleiadians all day.

Double cue screw face up

Okay then.

I would always wonder if it was just me. That I never felt a resonance with anywhere other than our planet. Okay, for you flat-earthers, which for me is a whole other book conversation in itself, I don't believe in one or the other. I believe in what is in front of me at this moment. I have never felt more of a connection anywhere other than our planet, Mother Earth. For the sake of terminology for the rest of this book, I will flick from planet to earth, realm, Mother Earth, Goddess, and back again. They all have the same meaning: the land under our very feet.

Here. Mother Earth. Our planet. This realm, with the red earth and grass beneath my feet, with the salt water splashes, sand, and dirt between my toes, and the brush of the cool air on my skin, with the warm sunning rays burning away any bugs right deep into and through my blood.

Here.

This Earth.

This Home.

This place. This dirt. This Realm.

The ground under your feet.

The ground under *our* feet.

I love stargazing and have always been fascinated by the stars, even as a kid. But my 'home' has always been this earth. This Mother. This realm. Here.

I was born in the desert, in the Australian Outback. I came from the Red Earth Centre, literally, from what was the second-biggest bustling outback town aside from Sydney in its heyday of the early 1900s.

I am one of the Ancient Blooded Healers who came from the moment time began on Earth.

It would always fascinate me how people would talk of galactic star homes, and I would just be like, 'Ergh, but we are here, on this Earth, from here,' and shrug my shoulders and just listen, and it would never make sense to me. It never resonated with me. The idea that we come from—and should be—anywhere other than here, with our feet on this ground in this realm, is what causes the hallucinogenic disassociation of our human body. 'Longing for Home' is the disconnection and dissociation from your physical body and from the connection of the earth beneath your very feet.

This realm is in my blood. It is in OUR blood. Last time I checked, I am sure you are as human as they come.

As Ancient Blooded Healers, we ground people. We bring people back to Earth. We get them out of their heads and into their hearts, and most don't like that feeling.

They would rather stay in their heads, connected to their star lineage, and not come to Earth. But there is a reason they did. There is a reason they are in a human body on this earth, walking the grounds that they are with a human heart.

We are Ancient Blooded Healers.

We have walked this land since the dawn of time.

We did not come from some other galactic race; we are the mother fucking galactic race; we are from here, from EARTH. Our bloodline is deeper than this earthly realm. It is all combined in multiple multi-dimensional convergence layers of generational soul tied through consciousness. This is our lineage. This is our realm, and it is here that all of the inter-convergence comes together to be US.

We Are Consciousness.

Trying to embody or think you are from some far-off other galaxy is a disconnect from your true and highest self—from being human. From being real. From Feeling. From Being HERE. From your *Heart*. You are born of the earth and will return to the earth; you have been here since the dawning of time.

Ancient Blooded Healers are incredible shapeshifters; we absorb and can become any lineage, realm, or galactic being as fast as a thought and receive upgrades, downloads, information, and healing, but we are not them; we are us, the Ancient Blooded Healers. Your lineage is here, in this realm, on Earth, in the place beneath your feet. It is a deep part of our gift to be able to do this; that is why they come to us and want to study us—we are different, gifted, and have been headhunted for eons of time. We are the technology.

Listening to other galactic stories and trying to find where you came from or belong keeps you trapped in the cyclic loop of dissonance and distortion and out of connection with your highest self—out of connection with YOU. Out of your heart. Out of this Earth. If they keep you focused on something outside of this current reality, well, you will miss what is going on right under your feet in this reality, right?

Remember that your connection to your highest self is your power, and they don't want us in our power, do they?

Who is 'they'?

Any power above us. The ones that 'control' society.

The ones that cut off our voices and silence us.

The 'spiritual gurus' keep you out of this realm of reality.

Sure, the 'big guns' of the world are only toys at the top level. It is bigger than us and than them. They just don't burn us at the stake these days, but they used to. Today, they still do—just in other forms and ways.

Oh, and by the way, 'they' is an aspect of your consciousness and psyche, and *that* is the only thing holding you back from the Ancient Blooded Healer lineage of your power that is here to change the world with your being.

Trying to find your lineage and your home anywhere other than where you are right now gives 'them' your power. You will feel trapped, stuck, paralysed, and in fear, focused on what 'they' are doing to society and 'how bad it is'. This is the dissonance loop; with deep aspects of your own power, they hold you captive here, which can freeze you or...

Free You

You are from here. You are an Ancient Blooded Healer. The faster you accept and deeply come back into your grounded truth about that, the faster you can heal, get on with your unique purpose, and finally live your life instead of hiding behind some facade, thinking this is your life. Let alone freeing humanity. The very thing you're angry about is what 'they' are doing to 'us'. Let's be real. I guarantee you're not happy holding some mask up, pretending this is what you asked for, because reality is showing you something different than what some 'manifestations' are supposed to have been by now.

Think about it. Who are the ones telling us we came from any other place than where we are?

The ones wanting to keep you stuck, sick, and in a cyclic 'where am I?' lost space, so you don't take back your power!

No one truly knows the ancient history of civilization. There are many people trying to piece it all together 100%. However, nobody truly knows where we came from or what exists out there.

The reason you have always dreamt of high-class luxury—the reason it has always been in your soul longing—is that your true orientation lineage is that of your Ancient Blooded Healer lineage. You were not a peasant. You were not just an herbalist. You know magic. You know, inter-dimensional language. You know, healing. You are bathed in rich metals and deep stonework, and you are made of them. You are the technology. You are powerful beyond measure, and it is NORMAL.

Our realm has been decimated, pillaged, and destroyed.

This book is dedicated to helping you take back your power, reclaim your sacred heritage, and release the patriarchal, chastising, hateful sinner energy and programming out of your system. Collectively, we were not only burned at the stake, but our consciousness was wiped clean—wiped only to remember what they want society to remember.

In December 2018 and January 2019, I kept receiving messages that Lumeria and Atlantis were rising. What I was sensing is that the

The Truth Is Rising.

The Truth Cannot Be Suppressed Any Longer.

As I always say,

You Can't Stop Consciousness From Awakening.

Then 2020 happened, and they tried to lock us down. That lockup awakened many. For the first time, everyone was able to STOP. REST. Change life's direction. It was a wake-up call for many and has caused a dramatic and rapid shift in consciousness in our realm. Many truths surfaced and continue to surface out of the deeply buried truths—about Atlantis, Lumeria, and our Ancient Realm buried under our feet. Or are layers of consciousness buried beneath our feet?

The Consciousness of the Old Realm, of our Ancient Realm, of our home that was decimated and pillaged and is covered up left, right, and centre, that so many of us long for, is awakening.

The Garden of Eden is real; it is here, on every ground we walk upon, on every inch of land in this ancient land under your feet. It is not compartmentalised into one tiny bit of our earth, but our entire earth. The Mists of Avalon, Atlantis, and Lumeria were our entire waters and lands before they were invaded, pillaged, torn apart, raped, and destroyed.

Have you always felt like any work you do would be taken away? Or fear that your children would be taken away from you? Or that you would lose the very thing that matters most to you? Or that your entire world or life would be destroyed if you ever got what you really wanted? Or are you scared of water or drowning? While there are many layers here, and childhood traumas definitely play a role in this, this is a collective remembrance of the truth of the decimation of our realm. When you feel these fears overwhelmingly at particular times in your life, know that you are awakening to another layer of truth; an old trauma and memory are surfacing.

Ancient Blooded Healer, you are awakening, and this book is a guide to support you in your journey to remembering who you are and becoming the truth of who you are.

This is your permission slip to trust yourself and your wisdom and to stop looking outside of yourself for any sort of validation, confirmation, or guidance other than your own internal self.

Stop looking for signs.

From even Angels.

Or even feathers.

Even myself.

Even the book you read.

Even the course you took.

Even the show you watch.

Even the teacher you studied under.

Even the Guide that came to you in your dreams and told you such and such.

Or the Star Being visit outside your window that night.

Now, I LOVE Angels, work with them daily, and could and do talk about them until the cows come home. I love feathers, signs that fall in my lap, and numbers that cross my path right when I want to give up and walk away from it all.

SIGNS ARE IMPORTANT!

Contradictory, I know, right?! Bear with me here...

Angels, Spirit Guides, Mentors, and any Being or sign that comes to you—sure, you can learn from them, grow with them, and expand your consciousness. It *is a stage of your Spiritual Awakening to open up to them, listen to them, and learn from them.* It is an avenue for training your psychic abilities. But they are not superior to you. You hold just as much power as they do; *you just haven't permitted yourself to be at this level of power yet.*

Angels, Spirit Guides, or any other Galactic Being are no different from me or another human teacher, book, class, or course telling you, sharing with you, or teaching you anything.

If you're reading this book or have picked it up, it is because you are ready—you have reached a level of mastery in your spiritual evolution and your soul's journey where that is enough to reach for anything outside of yourself.

It is time to take back your power, dear Ancient Blooded Healer.

This book is your permission slip (not that you needed it, but now you have it, so no excuse) to own the fuck out of who you are.

Your lineage.

Your too muchness.

Your feeling different from anyone else in the room, group, or family.

You will take bits that you resonate with, walk right the fuck away from anything else, and follow your true-hearted self the entire way home.

You have internal guidance and wisdom inside of you. You are not from some far-off planet or galaxy that no longer exists.

You are here; it is right beneath your feet—it always has been—as an Ancient Blooded Healer, and you have walked this earth since the dawning of time.

I See You.

I Honour You.

My intention for you in this book is that you come into such a deep love for who you are—for the gift, the magic, and the divine essence of who you are—that your entire life changes to be that of love because you have come home to yourself and realised...

Who You Are.

Now, let's do this.

Chapter 2

The Makings of An Ancient Blooded Healer

You are different. You always have been. In school, growing up, early adulthood, and later adulthood, you've always felt different. It is because you are. There is nothing wrong with you; you are an Ancient Blooded Healer, and you have a Gift, a Lineage, and a Purpose, which is why you have always felt different. You're here to create *massive* change in this world. You are part of a Consciousness that is here to affect mass Consciousness on a global scale that ripples through the Universe, changing the course of the trajectory of where we are headed. You are here to accelerate the growth of Human Consciousness because you are way more advanced than you give yourself credit for, which explains why you always feel like you never fit in. It's time to own your power about this. You're ahead of your time because you're here to lead the way, to guide others, and to create global change. You're a Leader.

That is why everything appears wrong to you. People call you 'controlling' because you always go in and make everything better than when you left it. You're just putting things in an order that makes common sense, and you don't know why they don't do it in the most efficient way possible. You have often wondered why and how they would do it any other way because you always find the flow to be the fastest, most efficient, and most practical way to do things. You're so connected to it because you're an extension of it. While everyone is, you're conscious of it and naturally connected to it; it is your natural talent and ability.

You're a high achiever. You always got top grades, and you still do. You excel at anything you do. You're constantly learning, no matter how old you are or whether you're doing it for a certificate or not. You will do anything you need to do at the last minute because, well, why would you do it any other way? While people have labelled this a trauma response (which I call bullshit), it is also the most effective use of time and energy. You navigate Consciousness, energy, and flow as one of your natural talents, skills, and abilities, and you wouldn't do it any other way.

You advance in your career faster than anyone and always climb the ladder right to the top without even trying, even though you give it your all at the same time. You rarely work for someone else; you usually have your own business. You value your freedom that much, and if you work for someone, you're the one managing everyone and being given the keys to the kingdom. You are given a lot of responsibility in your role. Or, you have created and attracted a job that you can pick and choose your own hours. You are always prepared for anything; you always have what you need at any given time. You are rarely without and always attract what you need when you need it. This is normal for you.

You do whatever it takes. You don't even think about it half the time. You hold the household together, the business together, the family together, and somehow look after yourself (more often than not just, if not at all, but fast learn that doesn't work for long). You do extraordinary things that are out of this world to other people, and when they say it to you, you don't even blink an eye (it's normal, right?), but also, in those moments, you realise just how much you hold all on your own. You're an efficient multi-tasker and do it effortlessly with grace and ease; it's something you don't even think about.

You talk to yourself. You think things out aloud, talk things out aloud, and figure things out aloud! This is normal until someone points it out, and you realise it again. And yet, you don't care, of course. But it is something that is so normal to you. Especially when you're concentrating on something, learning something new, figuring something out, replaying that conversation or situation that you're sure your intuition is correct on, or you want to ensure you are doing something correctly. (Don't interrupt my concentration flow!)

You say yes and figure it out later. You take risks that are normal to you, and others wouldn't even dare even think of throughout their lifetime. And yet again, it is normal for you. You think bigger than most, have a huge concept of how reality works and functions, and are very apt at jumping on new opportunities that fulfil your heart and are deeply soul-fulfilling. Things always work out for you (not that it is the easy road, that is for sure!). You have a lot of trust in yourself and the Universe to guide you through each step. When opportunities arise, you say yes. Even though to someone it looks like you didn't think about it and are being 'illogical or radical', you've been ready for a long time because things always work out for you. You know an opportunity combined with divine timing when you see one.

You live a very different life, even though it is normal to you. The ones that have set themselves free will be on the healing path. You're told you're a free spirit; sometimes you own this, and sometimes it wakes you up again, realising how different you are from normal society. You are usually always studying or obsessed with some kind of healing modality, creating your own modality, building your business, or creating your art. You live for this every single day with gusto and passion! (Why wouldn't you just? Isn't this normal?) If you haven't already got your own business, you're starting your own business because working for anyone else is suffocating to your soul, and you were born for *freedom,* baby!

You are stronger than most. You have been through the wringer and some and are somehow still standing. You are not sure how people don't get it, but you also realise that they will NEVER understand what you have been through. You have given up trying to explain and just smile and nod now, all the while feeling so different and like you don't fit in as much as you try. But you're at a point where you don't care if you don't fit in. You often don't realise how strong you are until someone points it out to you. Isn't this normal? You're ready to own your uniqueness and lead the pack.

You're smarter than most people. This is not from an egotistical perspective. This is something many Ancient Blooded Healers have stifled and shut within themselves; for those they were brought up around or spent time around, shut them down! Remember, you pick up other people's subconscious stuff; you tap into realms that most can't reach. You're highly sensitive to energy *and can usually* decipher it in the blink of an eye—more than you realise! This makes you highly affluent in sensing the fastest energetic routes that 'make sense'. You do this without even thinking about it, which is why hanging around the wrong people 'makes you stupid' because you begin to listen to them more than you do to yourself. If you've 'lost' this along the way, it's time to pick it back up (and reassess who you're hanging out with!).

You have an innate connection to Source that gives you this information, and for a long time, you just thought everyone was the same and could sense the same because it was so normal to you. You assume this is normal for other people. One day, you realise how different you are, and then you also start owning that. You hold a *power* that people feel. It's your energy. They are not looking at you; they are looking at your energy. It is this innate source connection that they feel. It is why they mostly run from you. It is why they call you crazy when you simply pick up on subconscious stuff they are unaware of. This is your gift. You're emotionally intelligent, and it is your heart energy that you are a 'genius' in. You're intuitively smart. That is a threat to people who need and require logic to figure things out. Be your intuitive, smart, genius self and own it anyway.

You always feel out of place; you never fit in anywhere you go. No matter how much you work on your self-development to accept the fact that you are different, there are times that you feel more out of place than others. You're a really good chameleon—you can talk to anyone, you fit into any group if you have to, you slip and slide in here and there, but you still always have that undertone feeling of 'I don't belong here'. You go to bed night after night, wondering how this will ever change. You enjoy your own company and accept your aloneness, but you also wonder more often than not. That feeling always lingers there. This is because you are a leader, and you're not born to fit in. You're here to contribute to the mass awakening of Consciousness in this realm. Get cosy with other leaders doing the same, and you'll find your tribe, your place on this earth, and your reason for living. Step into your Leadership role now; do not delay this one more day. This is what you were born for; it is time to come out of the spiritual closet.

One day, a switch will come internally, and it no longer feels like a displacement; it becomes your ally, your best friend, and you realise it is your power. It is yourself that you have been pushing aside to try and fit in, and this is the biggest abandonment feeling you could possibly ever feel. You may be lost in grief, pain, anger, hurt, and betrayal, wondering how you will ever get out of it. Well, there are times when you wonder why even bother because there is no point, no reason, to do any of this anymore. But this is because you have evolved and shifted. You are only keeping yourself in situations where you stay small, afraid of shining the truth of who you really are, hanging around people who also keep you small—even unconsciously.

One day, there will come an internal switch, and you will realise that there has been no one else like you along your journey until this day, that you have always felt out of place, no matter where you are, and that this is a 'homecoming' to yourself. Suddenly you feel connected to everything and everyone once again, and thank fuck for that. It's like you've been down the biggest black hole ever, and you are starting to climb up, stair by stair, rock by rock, breath by breath, and you are slowly (or fast!) coming out of the big hole you've been in. It can feel like waking up all over again. It can feel like you've been reborn. Some people call this coming out of the Dark Night of the Soul. And yet, this time, you're coming out different. You're not the same anymore. You're not in Kansas anymore. Your mind, body, and heart have been altered, and you are walking forward now with so much wisdom that was an essential part of your life purpose, activating into deep alignment for the role you are here to walk on this Earth. You have a lot of life experiences under your belt, and not many walk through what you've walked through. There is a reason for that. Dear Ancient Blooded Healer, you're a Leader; you're here to contribute to the Awakening of Mass Consciousness in this realm in a big way. Yes, I think this is the third time I have said it. Are you getting it yet?

You have been through the biggest initiation of your life. There is a LIFE-CHANGING, Soul-Shaking, Life-Purpose-Awakening reality shift when you reach this moment. You have walked through the biggest Dark Night of the Soul and initiation of your life, and you are completely reborn.

You reconnect with yourself; you remember who the fuck you are, and you come home. You channel that divine energy of yours into your true, unique Life Purpose instead of trying to fix everything and everyone in that insatiable, energetic, ungrounded, erratic mess. You hone that baby all the way home to your unique gifts, skills, and abilities and finally do what you were born to do. By the way, energetic, ungrounded, erratic mess is welcome here; that is where the best fire creation is born. This is a sacred part of you. It is just about channelling it through your Life Purpose Mission, and one day, it *clicks*, everything makes sense, and you become on FIRE with your true God-given Life Purpose illuminated path.

You have an Affinity with Stones, Rocks, Crystals, Candles, Aromatherapy, Scents and Smells, Feathers, Animals, Bones, Oracles, and Tarot Cards. Affinity? You can't get enough of them! You would be happy in a little forest cabin with only these things! You drool over smells; you have a collection of stones, crystals, feathers, or teddies. Teddies are alive for you. In fact, everything is alive for you. Even rocks and teddies have feelings. You have always felt this way about things that others look at you strangely for. Oh, and fire and some good wild-foraged food. And let's not forget all your animals. At the same time, you love the finer things in life because you're also aware it is the 21st century, so you pull yourselves back from those timelines and enter into now. You love luxury, being provided for and having everything you need at your fingertips. Ancient Blooded Healers are also very practical and efficient, having everything on hand, no matter what astrological star sign you come under.

You also know that you can have the best of both worlds because you know, realise, and live the fact that on this Earth, in this realm right now, you could have your off-grid forest cabin on sacred acreage hidden away from the world. You could have a lush, luxe, deeply held, nourished, supported, and convenient lifestyle. In fact, you realise that time travel is real because, at any given moment, somewhere on this planet, in this realm, we have access to all of this. We have it all right here, beneath our very feet.

You Make Potions. You may do this for work, have created a business out of it, or used to do it as a kid. Or you may have a lot of potions, incense, and candles and love different creams, lotions, and smells! Your sense of smell is so clear and strong for you. You even smell intuitive smells—Clair smells—very clearly. When I was little, I made all kinds of stews and concoctions from leaves, berries, sand, rocks, and even bits of plastic pipe when I was at my dad's work as a child. 'Pipe stew'. I used to make it for my teddies.

Today, you still brew teas and other 'potions,' and you have fond memories of making potions and stews with different 'ingredients' too. You are of the Ancient Blooded Healer lineage, I tell you! You have an innate ability to mix just the right amount of different things. When you cook, you frequently cook intuitively without measuring, and it turns out amazing. You can make the same meal repeatedly, but it usually tastes different every time you make it because of your intuitive potion-making flow each time you do. You 'just know' when food is ready and rarely use a timer. When you forget about the food and rush to the kitchen stressing out because you forgot about it, but it... 'Oh, it is just perfectly ready!' And then begin to realise you're not rushing to the kitchen because you forgot about it; you just remembered it because your intuition just told you it was ready! Ah, the relationship learning we go through with our intuitive communication!

You Return Your Blood to the Earth. You connect deeply with Ancient Ritual; even though you may not know much about it at this moment (or you may be engrossed in it), it fascinates you. You connect with your womb magic, blood cycles, and menstrual PMS. You have a strong affinity for herbs, minerals, spices, and the throws of the deep forestry and watery lands of Avalon, Lumeria, Atlantis, Tartaria, the Worlds of the Old, the Ancient Realms, and the Moon Cycles, which you know are still very alive and accessible today. Even if only the names sound familiar. If you're a male reading this, you admire Intuitive Priestesses and are drawn to Wizardry, Magic, Spiritual Warrior Training, Man's True Purpose, and Ravens. You know you're highly intuitive; the cycles and rhythms of everything that makes up life deeply nourish and fascinate you, let alone make you very apt at working with them. You've always been different from the 'boys', even though you have fit in over the years because, you know, chameleon and all. Whether you live in a city, on a farm in the country, or high up in the mountains, you have your own rituals that are strong, ingrained, and deeply natural to you. They would be like miracles if mainstream people used them. You recycle and use everything in a particular item instead of throwing it out half-used; you see how to 'use it all'. You return anything to the earth that you can and dispose of other things in ways you know are the fastest and most efficient.

You're Connected to the Seasons. You're very aware of the change in Seasons; let's be real, you're so aware and sense the slightest change in the Earth's atmosphere and weather, let alone the Seasons. You're very connected to how the Seasons affect you, and you are deeply honoured by each phase. You notice how much the Seasons have changed over the years, yet you honour each phase—the equinoxes and the solstices—and are deeply connected to 'time' via the seasons of the year, the moon phases of the month, and the sunlight hours of the day. You relish putting blankets, rugs, and other winter pieces out in the spring and summer warmth and celebrate the shift that comes around to mark a new dawn. You love planting in your garden in time with the natural cycles and are deeply connected to this ritual, whether you consciously do it or not or even plant a garden. You're conscious of the seasonal foods and the time of year via the Seasons. You plant, grow, and dry herbs and other foods that you store and use seasonally. You're deeply in tune with these rhythms.

Cleaning and Organising Relaxes You. Only in flow, though! Otherwise, you get angry if you force yourself to do it when it is not in flow or aligned! You will constantly clean if you are avoiding or unsure of your Purpose. You will make it a priority and 'all you do'. However, if you are working on channelling your Purpose in whichever way, shape, or form, cleaning is only done in flow and done in the most efficient timeframe because you're trusting flow timing when you do it (not something you really think about; you just do it and usually realise after 'why'!). You love having a cleaner and someone to take care of essentials like this; however, there comes a point where you need to do it yourself. It is the energetic clean that you work on, and it feels so different to do it this way. You're conscious of how much cleaning and clearing with an energetic intent shifts energy and changes the entire feel of your home. You can literally change your mood (and life!) when you do this, and you're super conscious of this. It is important to you. You may use Feng Sui or know where a certain placement of items belongs because you feel it. In fact, you don't think much about that either; you just do it, and it feels amazing.

You Have a Strong Connection to Children, Even If You Don't Have Any. Children always look at you, connect with you, and even want to climb all over you! In a crowded dinner party, you'll be the one who ends up connecting with the children most of the time. They will seek you out, and you just seem to know how to make them feel welcomed, loved, and connected in a room that doesn't seem to understand them. It is like you have an unspoken language for understanding them, and that connection is real. People will leave their kids with you all the time. It is okay to set boundaries and not care for other people's children, okay? You have your own life to live, and as much as you love them, it is okay to say no. You may have a strong calling to 'save the children' or have always felt that you would work with children in some way concerning your Life Purpose, even if you are unsure how. Maybe you already do.

You Have a Strong Connection to Nature and Animals. You're deeply in tune with the cycles of Nature and love the shift in seasons. Even though you prefer to be in a warmer climate most of the time, you're savvy to the cold and icy winds. You hear the trees talk, see faces in the rocks and stones or water droplets in the shower, and hear the flowers speak. You see the fairies in the trees and the glimmering light, and you watch the dragons and angels take flight in the clouds above. You are so deeply connected to water and its mysteries that you could stare at it for hours and not be bored. In fact, you do.

You sense the energy and cry when trees are cut down because you not only feel their pain—honey, you're feeling the pain of when our original lands were destroyed and the trees bigger than the tallest buildings on Earth were destroyed. That pain is as ancient in your blood cellular memory as you are. You literally feel the vibrations of the earthquakes in the country next door, let alone the mining that rocks the ley lines of the lands you feel. You are *highly* sensitive to the slightest vibrations, so subtle and deep, of the changing shifts of the Earth's atmosphere.

I was devastated when, shortly after moving into a place where I had lived for eight years in 2012, they cut down two huge tea trees in the backyard. I was so upset. One morning, after my big, grieving, deep tears at their loss, I was in the kitchen, and all this light beamed in from the sunshine that hadn't come in before due to the trees. It was here that, even through the pain of losing our best friends (the trees), that light shined deep into the darkest crevices to heal core wounds. That home and my time there was a huge healing portal for me and created a safe space where I stepped into Reality Awareness, from just a few workshops and the odd client in person to the foundations of the online empire you see today. I wouldn't be here without that Light beaming through that place at that time. Even though they were cut down almost immediately after I moved in, those trees somehow healed me.

Another time, when I was 14, I used to walk my dog every day after school to get out of the house. I would walk through this particular bushland, and one day, after not walking that way for some time, I came across the entire bushland having been bulldozed down and being marked out with pegs and tape for housing development. I stood in shock at the cleared land and then burst into tears and anger as I went through and ripped out all the wooden peg markers and tape. I was so devastated that they had destroyed the forest, even though, at that age, I didn't quite understand why I felt so strongly about it, except for the fact that you don't destroy forests! I definitely did not have the understanding back then that I do today. It was another seven years before I had my spiritual awakening.

Animals are always around you. You've always had a lot of pets. Pets and Wild Animals come to you. They cross your path. People give them to you. You breed them. You'll be driving down the road, rescuing lost pets and keeping them until their owner returns from work, or you put them back where they live. Animals are drawn to you; they listen to you, and you hear them speak. You know what is going on for them, and you can sense the connection to their owner like you're talking to a person. Wild Animals come to you, and you're like a walking Shaman with your connection to the animals you find anywhere, including on the main street in the city! You rescue wild animals and take them to Animal Shelters if you don't care for them yourself.

You don't always have to rescue the Animals that come to you. When I was 28, I stepped into teaching workshops and classes in person in a bigger way, expanding my business. I became really busy learning a whole new system for 'how to do this'. Then, all of a sudden, every day, there would be a lost dog or an animal that needed rescuing. Or a bird that would literally fly at my feet, and I would set up a cage, take it inside, nurture it, and it would die. This would happen repeatedly all of a sudden. I realised a few things in this space. Birds or animals that would come to me and die not long after—I helped them cross over. I gave them a safe space to die rather than leave them alone in the wild. I also realised that *a part of my life was dying*. It was an old cycle that was closing out, and my life would 'never be the same again'. 28 is also the 'Saturn Return', so it was a significant time of my life, no doubt, but expanding my business and new learnings were definitely a huge structural change on many levels.

At this time, I had a chat with Archangel Ariel, the overseer of animals. I told her that she needed to find someone else to take care of these animals if I was to do the work in the world that I knew I was meant to do and that I had just stepped into and started to work every day. I didn't have 3-5 hours or more to contact owners and hold their pets until they got home, rescue wild birds, keep them and care for them, or drive them to the wildlife caregivers. I may as well have been talking to people on the phone all day, taking up my precious time. Even though I loved my friends and family, I was starting to get serious about building my business, and I had to set some solid boundaries. It is okay to do this, by the way! Whether with family, friends, or the animal and spirit worlds, it is essential if you are to break out of the old systems and create something new in the world, your life, your business, and what is trying to pour out of you—it is okay to say no, so you can say yes to you and your Purpose!

Of course, I could've kept doing this. I love animals, after all! However, I knew it was taking up time that wasn't my overall role or purpose and was pulling me away from what I knew I was truly meant to be working on in Reality Awareness. I am sharing this to let you know that when you step up to your Life Purpose Mission work, you will find that life *will* become chaotic.

All of a sudden, there will be all this other shit to deal with in your life that you did not have before. Relationships can crumble or go through their own rebirth as you shift to another level together (this is just all the crap being cleared out). You will have more tasks to do that have nothing to do with what you need to do or that you were about to step into doing, even though they can look like signs you are 'meant to do' (see my animal experience, for example).

All this teaches you to stay true to yourself, maintain integrity, and implement strong boundaries. It is okay for you to say no, even though you may love it (me and my animals!), but I knew it wasn't my overall purpose or what I was bringing to the world. There are others in the world whose dedicated purpose is to care for animals. They wouldn't dream of doing anything else. It is important to know what you are being called to do and what is a distraction from what you are really meant to do.

Once you step onto a new path and dedicate yourself to changing your life, trust this process, trust yourself enough, and know it is okay to say no to things you love when you know it is not what you are meant to be doing. You will know because you'll feel agitated and (slightly or significantly) resentful doing it if you are not focused and spending dedicated time doing what you are truly called to do. Sure, I could've done both and made sure I put consistent effort into Reality Awareness as well as rescuing animals. But I chose not to. I didn't *want* to rescue animals all the time. This is your permission slip and 'okay' to not do all the things the Universe puts on your plate. It is okay to delegate, even by calling on the archangels or spirits to help you, as I did with Archangel Ariel. It is okay to say no to things you love so you can focus on what is really important to your mission and that you know you need to stop putting it off.

It doesn't matter where you are; Animals always show up. When you are working with a client, speaking with a friend or family member, or just in public in general, animals are always around. They speak with you constantly. I remember being in the city with my partner at the time, my daughter, and her friend. It was a Friday evening, and people were everywhere. It was nighttime, and we went for a walk after dinner before we left. We were walking down the main street, and I just happened to look up as we walked under trees in the centre, and there were huge white Ibis in the trees resting. I began laughing and walked right out from underneath them—it wouldn't be good if one of those shat on you! Everyone moved out of the way, and I couldn't stop laughing! I mainly laughed at how my innate connection knew they were there. There we were in the busy city, so far from the country, and there was not an animal to be seen on a busy Friday evening in city life, and I just happened to feel the Ibis sitting there in silence. It was as if they spoke to me and told me. I felt them; the connection was so strong. This is what you do—you just sense, know, feel, and can speak to animals telepathically and psychically, which is normal to you.

As an Ancient Blooded Healer, you feel and telepathically know animals are around. You just knew a snake was in the grass before you saw it. You can feel the shark in the water while surfing before you see it. You can hear the trees speak to you as if a person were standing there. You just know what an animal needs and can tell the entire family situation that the pet lives in just by communicating with the animals of the human family or the ley lines of the land.

When you lose an Animal, it is like losing a Human—worse! That is a big call to make, but for Ancient Blooded Healers, it is a thing, and it is huge. Whether you're an Ancient Blooded Healer or not, animal loss can make your entire world fall apart. What is important to understand is that when we lose an animal that became our best friend, if we look at 'when' we got the animal originally and what was going on in our lives when that animal came into our lives, most times, we weren't 100% in a good place when we did. We will be grieving the turmoil that was occurring at the time we got the animal. Our animal or pet came in at that particular time of our lives, healed us, and quelled the pain of that time. When the animal is lost or passes away, we are now in a place where we can deal with the trauma of the original wound that the animal or pet came to heal at that time in our lives. We were not capable or ready to deal with it back then, but when an animal passes or is lost, it is our time to heal, not just from the loss of our best friend but from that time in our lives. For example, you go through a breakup with a partner you thought you were going to marry. You buy a puppy, and not long after that, it becomes like your shadow, which you take everywhere with you. 10-15 years later, that dog passes away, and you're the biggest emotional mess ever for a long time and don't seem to get over it. Of course, you're grieving your dog, but underneath? It is the loss and grief of the partner you thought you were going to marry but didn't. Hence, the 'double-layered' grief that feels like your world is ending and some. Be okay with the deepest, sobbing grief you feel; sometimes you can't even take another breath. You are healing more than you are aware of. You're safe as you go there with this level of grief.

You Eat Meat. Right after we talk about loving animals, ha! The truth is, you're not concerned about eating meat or not eating meat. You are, and you aren't. You don't eat too much of it, but sometimes you do go through phases where you eat lots of meat. You will eat meat when your body craves it. Sometimes you only eat seafood. You're conscious of where you buy your meat from if you do eat it, and you choose organic farm-to-table where you can. You are very conscious of where your food comes from. You prefer to use the whole animal, and if you had the means to raise your own livestock and kill it yourself before you eat it, you would eat only the fish you catch and use the entire animal. This is your preference; should and could you. This is your Ancient Blooded Healer Soul. Most Ancient Blooded Healers possess these skills or know someone close to them who does. You are very practical, use everything that is necessary, and honour every part of the entire animal, including the entire process. That deep Ancient Ritual life, right?

Sometimes you eat meat, almost in shame and hiding, especially depending on who you have hung out with for a while. 'The modern-day spiritualist doesn't and isn't supposed to eat meat'. I call bullshit on that. Sure, you can go vegan and even breatharian; however, you know that you falter and get weaker at times if you do not include meat in your diet, even just in little bits through different phases of your life, especially motherhood. You honour your body and intuition more than you care to think what others think is true to you, especially when they don't know you, your life, or your body, so you carry on as the Ancient Blooded Healer Soul that you are.

You don't resonate AT ALL with modern-day slaughterhouses and the way that mainstream butchery is kept, and you know 99% of the population wouldn't eat meat if they saw in front of their eyes how it was done. You also know that, most definitely, they wouldn't be able to kill, skin, clean, or properly prepare their own meats either. They wouldn't know what to do with the entire animal, and it would be wasted. They wouldn't have a clue or the stomach to do it if their lives depended on it.

You're aware of chemicals in foods and prefer not to eat them. You struggle to walk down the laundry aisle of the supermarket and have to hold your breath as you do because the chemical smell is so overpowering for you. However, you're also not anal when it comes to surviving, living, or enjoying the finer luxuries of life. You're not strung up on strict veganism, raw veganism, paleo, eating right for your type, or any other modern-day term someone has coined for marketing purposes. Although, when you do a detox, cleanse, parasite cleanse, or complete lifestyle change and overhaul, you're very strict about what you eat and put into your body. Most of the time, you eat clean, organic, healthy as fuck food where you can anyway. You eat healthier than most people you know. Most people call you all sorts of things and sometimes look at you weird for what you eat. But you do what you do because you know, and why would you do anything other than what feels right to you? Don't feel ashamed about eating meat. Veganism was created mainly through religions to keep people weak and followers. Don't feel ashamed for eating whatever you know is right for your body, especially if it makes you feel good, strong, and grounded—even if that is raw vegan! Any given diet and how you eat are right for you over your lifetime, and that can change depending on what you are going through, giving birth to, or living. Trust it.

Most of the time, you prefer Intuitive Eating.

You're not afraid of eating what you need or want to, for that matter. You're here to experience life itself. You know what your body thrives on and does not thrive on, so you choose accordingly. You are conscious of the season, cycle, and timing that you are in in different phases of your life and prefer to nourish your heart, body, and soul from this place rather than on a should-or-strict basis. You won't go into a tizzy if you have to eat whatever you need to when you can, for whatever reason. You're a transmuter; you transmute any energy, which includes what you put in your mouth.

You Don't Live in Fear; You Live in Your Power.

You've tried every health fad, diet, lifestyle choice, and way of living under the sun, and you always come back to what feels right for you. For some time there, I felt bad. I would always buy all these supplements and spend thousands at the naturopath and live blood analysis practitioner, only taking the supplements for a week or so if I was lucky. Then I would take them here and there only because I felt terrible that I just bought them all and stopped taking them, and then they just sat there in my cupboard! After a while, I just got used to it. Occasionally I would go to the supplement cupboard, but I still barely took anything, let alone consistently.

I would see mentors, practitioners, and leaders online harping on about how much you have to do with supplements, and they do, and I would stay quiet and wonder why I didn't for a few minutes, then forget about it again. My body just wouldn't. In 2021, I caught Medical Medium Anthony William live on Instagram, and he was talking about supplements. He was sharing how he is not loyal to one company, and if another company comes out better than what he has found, he will move to them. He mentioned this because every company on the planet puts fillers in their supplements, even the ones that don't say they do. They do it, and it is like an unspoken thing that these companies do. He continued, saying it is rare for a company not to do it, hence why he uses a particular brand—because they don't do the fillers.

Now, what blew me away was that ALL those years, I would think to myself that I was terrible for investing 'all that money' in 'all those supplements' just for them to sit in the cupboard and not be used. It was actually my intuition telling me this about the fillers! I think this doubly hit home for me because a mentor with whom I was in her mastermind, once shared a story of her doing a big detox, and this particular detox was to release all the stuck plastic and crud in your gut. She had shown what had come out: all the plastics, capsules, and whatnot, even though they were 'vegan' or 'good for you' ones. Still, they were stuck in our bodies or guts, no matter how much 'cleansing' you do. It was so fascinating to me.

Hearing Anthony talk that day allowed me to drop deeper into my intuition and trust myself more, no matter how much whichever guru would preach, teach, and sell their product. No matter how much shame I felt for 'not fitting into the group', I didn't follow suit and buy all the supplements the mentor was selling. There was a reason I was not called to take them all—even though I spent thousands on them and would wonder why, at the same time, my body would repel them. My body knew. I feel the energy in what I eat and consume. The energies have to be aligned, or I just won't. Same as skincare for me. It took me years to find a skincare line that I could resonate with and that just felt right. It is the energy. And energy is everything!

It is a bit like when clients come to me and tell me, 'Oh yeah, I have been getting the message to drink more water, but just don't.' When I ask them if it would be tap water they would be drinking and they say yes, I am like, 'Well! Your intuition is telling you not to. Hence, you don't! If it were pure glass-bottled spring water at your disposal, I am sure you would gun it down by the gallon! We all know how much tap water is not good to drink because it is full of chlorine, fluoride and goodness knows what else!' As highly clairsentient Ancient Blooded Healers, we 'do' so much intuition that we don't even realise we are doing it. It is important to let go of guilt and shame and regain the trust of your intuition. You do know. And you feel it in your bones.

You've Been Bio-Hacking Before It Even Had A Mainstream Name. You have been living this way or dabbling in it ever since you knew about it—before it was made more public by advertising and marketing. You have done these techniques naturally and haven't even considered them a health fad or bio-hack because this way of living is normal to you. Now you see people on this health trend and wonder what the fuss is about because, well, isn't this normal?

When you speak, people listen. You have a deep ancient knowledge inside of you that when you talk, people listen, some intently, others screw up their faces at you, and sometimes they tell you to shut up simply because they do not get it. You are deeper than most. You hold an Ancient Lineage inside your cellular blood molecular structure and are here to shine a light on the deepest and darkest aspects of the world. You're ahead of your time. You walk into a room, and everyone stops, can feel you, and senses your power—even if they are unsure what they are sensing.

You know what people need and want before they want and need it. You have a gift for seeing beyond what people need at the forefront of their being. You are the one that will stop a boat from capsizing in someone's life (figure of speech). You can see how the tower will crumble, and you are there to catch all the pieces as they fall or to guide them before they do. You have an uncanny ability to know what is going on for a person before they say it. Sometimes you will say it, and they will be shocked at how you knew that because they haven't told anyone, and other times they will think you're crazy and tell you that because that isn't the truth! However, lo and behold, days, weeks, and even months later, you were right, whether they told you or not.

You walk in the dark. You're comfortable in the dark, and you realise you have no fear of it. While most put up protection walls and turn away from it and shun it, you're the one there, picking the demons up off the ground and transforming them as you walk past them because you have walked this Ancient land longer than they've been around and you know the invasion was never their fault, Moana style. You know how to clean up the mess—transmute them back to their hearts—and you do so easily, wondering how people don't just do it. It's so natural and second-nature to you. You begin to realise how different you are when people aren't energetically cleaning up like you. (This is normal, isn't it?) Yes. Yes, it is, dear Ancient Blooded Healer.

When it feels right, you do it—even when it doesn't make logical sense. You're a person who doesn't even question doing something. You just do it. You say yes and think about it later. You always figure it out. You are a leader in some way, shape, or form. You lead the pack. You always make things happen. You organise things and people and are usually on the front lines, figuring everything out for everyone else.

People who can't control you will blame you. For everything, usually. They rarely look at their own part in it. Even if they do, it will be for five seconds or a once-in-a-blue-moon event. You are called stubborn by those who are losing their grip on you. You are told to 'stop causing trouble' or 'to look deeper in yourself as to why you are causing this issue' or 'don't you think if your own family hates you, that you are actually the problem' by those that are living out of integrity with their own lives that you are calling them out on. This is accentuated because you have lost the courage to walk away for good.

You are called 'controlling' by those who realise they are losing you as you walk away from the unhealthy, toxic situation. Once you've made the decision to leave, there is no going back. You give second chances, but you are never fully back in it. Once trust is broken, there is nothing that can repair it, no matter how hard you try. One day, you reach your limit and leave. Until you do, it is very easy to find yourself in less than satisfactory relationships, constantly walking on eggshells, second-guessing yourself, losing yourself, and not being your authentic self, let alone living your true authentic life. Until one day, you reach your tolerance level for living like that and truly begin to make changes—even when it is inevitably so hard to do so, one day at a time, you do.

You stand up to authority. You will hold your ground and not back down. You know what is right and wrong and what is happening in the world and to humanity. You will not bend or break when it comes to standing up for what you believe in. You will honour this and hold your ground until the end, no matter what it takes, because you know the truth about our world. You know what is real and what is not, what is out of integrity and what is not. You live for the truth and won't stand for anything that does not align with yours and that of humanity. You know that by holding your ground, you know they can't do anything to you, and if you would just hold your ground, there is always a way out and around what 'they' do because what 'they' do is not correct for humanity. You are here to break the systems, and you know that standing up for your truth, holding your ground, and creating the new is what you are here for.

You live for the truth. You can't not be in truth, so when people around you are out of integrity and not living this way, you struggle to be around them, and 99% of the time, you don't. When you do stay around it, you always feel like something is 'off' in you, your life, business, or other areas, or you start to get snappy, naggy, or super lethargic, even manifesting issues like fibromyalgia. As soon as you start being honest with the life you are really living and start to make changes, everything changes back to pure health and alignment. Keep speaking your truth. Don't let the naysayers or gaslighters get under your skin. You don't have to 'leave every relationship' (unless it is aligned for you!). The reality is that you just haven't found your outlet to speak your truth for your Purpose work. When you do, the need to call out every single person you come across dissipates, and you can 'be in the world' and have your outlet for your true calling to shift the world without looking like a crazy person. Crazy is okay and welcome here, but if you are to truly make an impact with your mission and your Purpose, the correct outlet for your message can make or break your path.

You hold a melancholic disposition. Whether you're a meat eater or a 100% raw vegan, you have a melancholic disposition. As much inner work as you do, as much as you stay positive and are frequently told you're one of the most positive people they know, melancholy surfaces in your quietest moments, sometimes even in the most joyous of moments. It is not that something is wrong with you or that you are sad and need fixing. It is just who you are. You are accustomed to walking in both worlds at the same time, the Light and the Dark, so you hold both extremes. You can be in a moment of pure, unadulterated joy and happiness while having such deep, welling grief and feeling it all at the same time, on the same day, in the same breath. This is normal for us. There is nothing wrong with you. This is a gift and a skill. Fine-tune it and own it.

I believe this is a trait of Ancient Blooded Healers because of our deep Ancient Lineage in our cellular blood memory. When controlling and governing bodies of the people take blood and DNA tests (or 'virus' tests—covid, anyone? My daughter had the test done so she could fly overseas to visit her father, and when I watched them swab her nose and mouth, I was like, straight up DNA test. Ridiculous!) or you willingly search your DNA on ancestry.com sites, they are looking for our DNA—the DNA of Ancient Blooded Healers. We are not only One of A Kind, but they are looking to see how many of us survived through the obliteration of the Old Ancient World we once were—of the Consciousness that still lives inside of us, that pulsates through our DNA Cellular Bloodline Molecular Structure, that pulsates and cannot die, that re-creates and re-grows who we are, that awakens with each breath, our Ancient Blooded Healer Lineage.

You transmute a lot of energy constantly. You can hold and transmute the entire scale of darkness and light in a matter of milliseconds and thoughts. You can constantly and instantly tap in and out of any situation and understand the deep energetics going on for a person, event, place, or thing. You tend to have a higher consciousness and perspective than most people you know. It is for this reason alone, let alone everything else, that for good health and mental well-being, you should find your energy-clearing practises, self-care, wellness, and joy practises and always make them a priority. My Clairsentient Sponge Clearing Meditation is a powerful transmuter of energies. It can be found in the Life Purpose Essentials Meditation Kit on my website.

You Feel Alone Most Of The Time. First of all, let me explain that there are different feelings of being 'alone'. We will go over these before we 'agree' that you feel alone most of the time.

Abandonment Alone:

This is the deep black hole feeling, where you don't feel you can come back from. This feeling is ripe and strong after a breakup with a partner or the loss of a loved one. And it can hang around for years and turn into depression and a loss of love for life—that you, 99% of the time, used to be the happiest one, the brightest one, the one everyone would turn to and say you're the most positive person they know. But this big black 'sink hole' makes you question everything, and most times, you don't even question anymore because you have given up.

The loss of a person, whether through death or breakup of any kind (intimate, family, friend, career, mentor), if you are constantly thinking about them and they are on your mind, if it is all you seem to talk about and focus on, and OMG! It is driving you insane. If you are still heartbroken about it all, it is because you haven't grieved for it yet. You're not over it yet. The way we 'get over something' or 'let go of something' is by actually feeling the depths of grief about the event.

The event could be fresh or have happened years ago, and yet, there are times when the grief hits you again like it was yesterday. This is normal. Grief comes in waves; this is normal. Grief is deep, no matter how long ago the situation was, as we can tend to bury things and get on with life fairly adequately as society has been trained like this. Grief comes in all shapes, sizes, forms, and feelings. It can be melancholy about the situation, anger, rage, remorse, bargaining (wishing you did this or that and then this wouldn't have happened), and of course, tears and deep, deep sobbing, which I call 'piercing the veils of grief'—the one where the howling grief is so deep, you don't feel you can take another breath. But you do—usually while lying on the kitchen or bathroom floor.

This abandonment feels like a big black sinkhole. It will be nothingness. You don't feel like your heart can take much more—every single moment—and in the depths of the waves of it, you will usually repeat this over and over again. I wrote a blog in August 2022 that explains it perfectly:

'When that wave of grief comes over you... when you are falling to your knees and want to be anywhere but HERE, and you are 'stuck here'—or can't—or plans are delayed... you are being faced with HERE...

There is a longing to get away. But it is like a tornado is ripping through your system, from the ground up, like someone lifting a cloak from you, up and out through your heart as it pours out with blood-lit tears on the floor, like you don't know if your heart can take much more...

Your entire energy system, aura, chakras—it is like a huge veil is being lifted from you when you are flooding on that floor and dragging your feet along once more because you can't do anything but be here with it.

And so, you walk forward, one foot dragging along to the other foot—one foot in front of the other...

As everything you've ever known is totally disintegrating from your being—your old life—you cannot return to it anymore.

That old life is gone. Gone. GONE.

And that is confronting.

The feeling is not even like there is nothing under your feet anymore.

Because you are very present. Here. With what is under your feet that you are dragging one foot in front of the other moving forward, you are just... here.

The grief is real because you are feeling it all, leaving your system, and arriving fully and completely HERE.

Self-care, filling your cup with things you once loved and relied on, hasn't been doing it for you lately, and that's also confronting.

You are being 'plodded' into a whole new reality right now.

You are being shredded from your old life, but you are so connected to right now, more than ever before, and receiving your right now...

You've... Surrendered and are very... Here.

You're... Being nourished by what is in front of you and the need to run away have lessened, gone even. You are finding solace in what is in front of you. You are realising... you're it... and starting to feel whole in this. You are receiving nourishment, self-care, self-love, and self-respect from your current reality. From... YOU.

You don't need to run anywhere to be filled up.

You are not jumping from thing to thing; you are stabilising a new frequency, that is...

YOU.

And that is a whole other level, whole other game, whole other integration you didn't see coming...

That broken heart that sent you into the deepest spin and journey of your life was only bringing you back to LIFE.

To YOUR life.

To... you.

And thank fuck you surrendered to it.

Abandonment Aloneness is the worst. It can come from a breakup or the death of a loved one. The deep core cause usually stems back to when you were a baby in the crib; however, it can also be from past lives. Even though every feeling is 'the worst' in its own accord, Abandonment Aloneness has a category all on its own.

Abandonment Aloneness can be labelled as 'victim'—'stop being a victim.' Gosh, it fumes me when I hear people say this. They, too, will never know the deep gift of intuition that the Ancient Blooded Healers have that this level of grief entails. Not many are willing to walk these depths of grief, but the Ancient Blooded Healers are. That is our playground. It is how Ancient Blooded Healers become and are so powerful in their gifts because they are not afraid to feel the depths of grief that most do not travel. Everyone wants to become more psychic, but not many are willing to feel the grief that gives them their gifts of being psychic.

By the way, someone 'being a victim' simply means they have not healed from the situation yet! Plain and simple! They are not doing it to get attention; they genuinely have not healed and are 'telling their story' because no one has truly been able to listen to them, hold space for them, or face the level of grief that is stuck inside there, deep inside that well of a black hole, and that is 'why' they haven't healed it yet. Hence, continue talking about it!

It 'plays like a broken record' because it is broken. There is a deep hole in the aura that the original trauma wound has created that hasn't been healed, felt, or dealt with yet. 99.9% of the time, it is not the person's fault. They simply have not had the right Healer or healing technique to be able to shift it for them. Remember, society has been trained this way because sickness and ill health are better for those in control at the top of the chain. It's not your fault!

Of course, they have to want to heal, but there is a misperception out there that they are simply staying stuck as victims because they want to. This is the farthest from the truth there is. They have not had someone who cares enough to show them how to heal or be there for them. More often than not, a deep mother wound sets the tone for the rest of their lives until they heal.

Abandonment Aloneness is the big black grief hole—a deep, immature space. Bear with me while I describe this. This isn't a dig at 'growing up' or 'stop being a victim!' (You know, I can't stand it when people say that! I just told you that.) This is deeply where, at this moment, you are in your Inner Child, and you ARE your Inner Child... and when you feel whole, complete, and loved again, that is when you have felt the depths of grief in this space. There is an aloneness that comes in here, where you have always been alone. It reaches a point where you do 'grow up' into maturity; however, that is different for everyone and depends on what kind of support, love, care, nurturing, and, most importantly, the proper healing and mentoring are around them. Some people never grow out of this immaturity because they don't have the right people around them.

The reason someone feels this black hole of abandonment and this level of grief—what feels like this hole that can never be filled—is because they are devoid of love. You have never actually had the kind, tender, loving care that you don't even realise is missing but is what is needed to heal. Ouch. That can be the harshest realisation that can sink one further because, well, if you have never had it, where on earth are you going to find it? The stark realisation can set off a new well of grief, and I want to say to you: go easy on yourself. Be gentle. Grieve and howl for as long as you need to. It will feel like everything is lost, there is no point, and just... WOW! I know this feeling, and I am here for you. You are not alone; there are MANY on the planet like us, which is why I am writing this book for you. You will get through this, but right now, there may be no light on the horizon, no matter which way you turn. Know that you are being recalibrated to an entirely different frequency, and soon you will have a new lease on life again. I know that might be hard to believe right now, but you will, I promise you. Give it a good few months (honestly, it takes time; hang in there), but you will. I love you.

You've Always Been Alone. Even in relationships, you have not felt 100% like you belong. You wonder if that is even a thing (to have the feeling of belonging) and constantly feel like your Soulmate is on the 'other side', helping you from afar, and that was your contract in this lifetime—to work from separate realms here. Your mission and purpose are strong, and you're willing to do it with or without 'a partner', so you do.

However, at the beginning of stepping into your Life Purpose, it is almost like you're waiting for your partner to show up because you feel you are supposed to do this 'purpose work together'. Then you realise it is you, or you submit to the fact they are 'on the other side'. You have tried all the manifesting techniques to call in the relationship of your dreams, then you let go and realise it is you and has been you all along, and then you get your purpose work done regardless.

What I have found fascinating about myself and many clients I have witnessed over and over again over the years is that they truly feel their partner is there, which is a big focus for a while, even calling him or her in. Then they feel them getting closer and closer. Then, usually, there is a big breakdown of some kind. Then, they 'all of a sudden' have clarity on their Life Purpose, breakthrough to a new level, and become known for what they do. This 'longing for a partner' is actually the longing for your own Soul, for your reconnection to the purpose of why you are here, why you were born, and why you are living. It's you that you've been waiting for. It is an incredible process to witness and so intriguing that after this big breakthrough, they no longer have so much attention on their 'long lost partner out there somewhere'. It literally was their clarity of Purpose coming towards them, or them towards it—their Soul grounding through them to earth.

You've always lived alone. You've always lived with someone or a family member, or you've always lived on your own the majority of the time, away from family, usually far away. Or, there has been a loss of contact when speaking to family, even if you are 'physically close'.

Alone in the Separation. There comes a point where you are connected to family and friends, but there is a separation. You outgrow people. You outgrow groups. You outgrow people you thought would be around you for the long haul. This usually happens quite quickly at certain times in your life. It is not only heartbreaking; it is excruciating. You think you are supposed to walk this spiritual path with someone. You wait and put off your Purpose because you are waiting for them to turn up to do it with you—because that is what you have always thought.

And then it gets to a point where you realise another year or five have gone by, and you surrender to this alone. You carry on with melancholy in your bones, doing your Purpose work. I do believe that there is someone out there for you. Don't stop believing because I don't, and I know there is, and it will happen one day. Believe.

Remember, You're One Of A Kind. There will be people who will NEVER understand. There will be MANY who will NEVER understand the true journey of an Ancient Blooded Healer and the level of 'aloneness' they walk. Even you wonder how you do it at times. You wonder if your heart can truly take much more because it just continues. And somehow, you continue. Some. How. You just... do.

Your Friendship Circle Changes Again and Again. You are usually a loner, and although you feel lonely sometimes—when you are truly honest with yourself, you also prefer your own company—you need lots of alone time to recharge. Every time you go through a shift, you notice the waves of not having friends—the friendship circles that drop or just don't resonate anymore. I thought it was weird not having friends. I just lived with it. It was normal to me.

I didn't think too much of it until a close friend told me, 'I don't have anyone else who is deep like this.' And that is when I realised 'why' I don't have a big circle of friends—because I only have deep friends, and at this point in time, there aren't many who are as deep as me in close proximity.

I could definitely go out and make friends and hang out with people, but I have realised that the deep stuff is where my heart is, so hanging out for the sake of talking about the weather doesn't do too much for me. I have always been alone in this way. I am always creating projects to support the consciousness of humanity simply because I thrive in this; it is Soul food for me. I am always the go-to person when someone needs healing. It is something I have become accustomed to as my role here on earth, and I am at peace with that. I also realised that I have many clients all the time. I don't have many 'friends' because my clients are like friends and are deep like me. I love my life, I love my work, I love the career I have created, and I love spending time with my daughter. I came to realise that it is okay to have a life you love that is different from the norm and be okay with that!

Over time, I realised there is a skill to being this deep, holding, knowing, and honing as much energy as we do. It is a skill to own your gift, to realise your depth, and to know who you are. Knowing the energy you bring to the table in any situation you place yourself in and what that does for people. Knowing when to speak, knowing what to speak about, and knowing to whom and when is a skill and a way of being. This isn't hiding who you are, but living your wisdom by connecting with humans. Being part of reality means being a part of life, not separate from it. Finding your place in the world means reaching a place where you don't feel like you don't fit in or don't belong because you have found who you are. The Aloneness Journey is so deep and dark that it eventually brings you here. Travel it until you reach here, because you will.

Alone with Boundaries. Along your journey, you will learn to define boundaries in different areas of your life. When you implement them—with fallouts, complications, doubting yourself, and knowing all at the same time that you cannot rise into the true Ancient Blooded Healer you are—with the life you truly want to live while not implementing these boundaries.

This will come with a good, hard look at yourself.

Who you are hanging around.

Who you still say yes to.

Who you still pander to.

It will reach a point where you feel rejected and alone because you are still in groups, hanging around certain relationships, or have just left groups or relationships and are questioning everything you did in that space. You will be looking back and realising they were the best moments of your life and that you learnt so many life skills that you will always cherish and still use to this day.

But you wonder how you could be so hurt in such a space at the same time.

This, *Alone with Boundaries*, is you stepping into your power, stepping away from what is no longer aligned, like truly stepping away, stepping into your self-worth, and what my mentor would call a 'tolerance shift'—of you not tolerating nor being treated this way for one moment more. 'ENOUGH,' as I would say. The snap has come.

You have come to a place where you TRUST yourself.

THIS is why it feels so hard. When you realise this, you can drop deeper into it, and everything else is irrelevant. It is okay to trust yourself on this one!

But for the next 18 months (roughly), it is usually a rough ride.

This snap is your Ancient Blooded Healer Soul.

Waking Up.

Waking up to YOUR truth, YOUR destiny, and YOUR way of life.

Most of the time, this realisation comes with a 'wake-up' call, and the confronting part is that what used to be aligned with your life—the way you live, post, talk, show up, or be in a relationship—is no longer congruent. The truly confronting part is not that you realise you're no longer that person, but rather, who are you now? Where do you go from here? How on earth do you get to where you know you need to be? But you also don't know where that is. 'How' trips you up because you've only done what you have always known until now, and now all that has changed, and—phew! Stop just for a moment. You *will* figure it out. You *will* be shown the way. But I guarantee you will feel lost for a while.

You can't move to this next phase without FULLY trusting yourself and where your intuition is leading you! Even away from the big, shiny objects!

I look back to the groups, family, friends, career paths, and relationships that I felt most rejected, kicked out of, and walked away from, shaking my head, not understanding what just happened and feeling so devastated at the same time, only to realise years later what really went on and why.

The women I felt most rejected by in the groups that 'appeared' to be my friends and then backstabbed me (the biggest reason I felt so hurt—that betrayal!) was because I didn't realise it until years later—ten years later! It took me quite some time to realise what was really going on, and it would happen over and over again until I realised it.

Once, I bumped into a woman at the supermarket; I hadn't seen her for 8–10 years. She burst out crying, telling me about the court order she had just completed due to the custody and domestic violence battle with her narcissistic ex-husband. She just blurted all this out to me, crying her eyes out as soon as she saw me—in the middle of the supermarket! I literally hadn't seen her for ten years! This is a family that had invited me several times to their home for dinner, and I was suddenly kicked out of the group we used to hang out in. I didn't know what was going on then and was so upset about it. Now I realise that the truth I brought up for people was just too much. It was never about me.

Another time, I had several women backstab me. I heard them through the grapevine. I walked away from those conversations, bawling my eyes out, not understanding what I had done for them to speak of me that way. Until again, several years later, we see that over half of them have separated from or divorced their now ex-husbands because of some level of domestic violence.

You see, who you are is TRUTH.

You live it.

You breathe it.

You talk it.

You walk it.

And that is triggering for people.

For many years, I walked around just living my best life with my daughter. Free, happy, and doing whatever the fuck we wanted when we wanted, much to the dismay of many people's judgments. I was happy and free in it.

At the time, I was also teaching Mums and Bubs Yoga and facilitating a Conscious Parenting Playgroup. We frequently talked about domestic violence and keeping ourselves and our children safe.

I forgot.

I forgot that all those years ago, I spoke about the *hard* topics and the biggest 'looking back now with a bird's eye view'. Many years later, in my online business with clients all around the world, I see that it takes time for one to wake up from a narcissistic, domestic violence relationship, then figure out what to do with that, and take action on that. It takes *years* for someone to go through this.

I didn't realise until years later that this was what was going on. I was triggering them with my truth—talking about these very truths! They knew it deep down but didn't know what to do with it, and then, over time, I guess it ate away at them enough to not live like that anymore, and they made changes, but it was me who brought that truth to the table and planted the seed. Not that I did it on purpose.

I was just being myself, living my best authentic, integrity-filled life, and that challenges people to live their own truths. It is something that, as an Ancient Blooded Healer, you learn to harness, hone, and channel in your life. You fine-tune your skills. It isn't easy. I went through so much realising all this and wondering what I did wrong until I realised this is who I am. I bring truth to the table wherever I go; it is who I am, whether I voice something or just my presence alone dismantles lies and betrayals.

It is here that we come to a different level of wisdom and power. There is nothing wrong with you. There has never been. You were just not given an instruction manual on what your very energy alone does to other humans.

You Have Transmuted Your Curse, Into Your Gift.

The Truth About Aloneness That Ancient Blooded Healers Feel. With all we have just talked about with Aloneness and the depth of the realisation of 'why' we feel this when I wrote about this very realisation for you here, I had the biggest shifts of my entire life. Everything moved rapidly after, and I not only realised this but wrote it for you here.

Are you ready for it?

The reason Ancient Blooded Healers feel so alone is that... **drum roll**

We Are So Connected To Everything.

Did you fall off your chair? Drop this book or device?

No. Probably not.

Writing about it doesn't seem as big as when the realisation dropped in.

But I hope it lands for you as it did for me without dropping your device in the process!

We are so connected to everything.

We feel everything.

Anything.

The slightest shifts in atmospheric energy. The neighbours next door. Your mother that is across the country. Your best friend on the other side. You feel it all.

Why?

Why do you feel that level of, like, everything?

It's because you're connected to it!

You're so connected to it—you feel so alone in it—because only other Ancient Blooded Healers have this level of connection to the earth we walk upon.

We are not taught any of this in school or during our upbringing. We are also taught not to feel on top of that! You know,

- Don't cry.
- Don't cry, or I will give you something to cry about.
- Don't show feelings.
- Don't talk unless spoken to.
- Listen only.
- Don't say what you really mean.

- Don't stand up for yourself.

I could go on.

And here you are, feeling EVERYTHING as a highly sentient being. So, of course, you're going to feel alienated, on the outskirts, and some because you feel so connected to everything! And isn't this normal?

It is strange to you that people can't feel the animals or the trees talking to them or see the sparkles of light of angels, orbs, fairies, and other realms open up like a doorway in front of them (and that is without any drugs or plant medicine, by the way). You don't need that stuff to see this; this is natural to you.

You are so connected, and between trying to navigate that and what society is trained not to feel or believe, well, no wonder you feel alone in the world!

Hopefully, not anymore.

Ancient Blooded Healer,

You Are Gifted.

You ARE the Unified Source Connection. It is why you change the energy of a room when you walk into it. It is why people look at you without looking at your hair! They don't know why they are drawn to you, stare at you, and 'just have to talk to you' because there is 'something about you' they can't describe or understand!

When you understand that your 'aloneness' is actually because you are so connected to everything and everyone, you reconnect to this Unified Source. You drop all the way back through the black hole—dropping, dropping, dropping—until you hit back into the pure light—the pure connection that is Source.

You reconnect. It isn't alone. It is a connection. Pure connection. Home. And in this place? Everything exists. You have everything you need, want, and desire, and you not only come back to life but also to your power because you remember the truth of who you are. You consciously connect to all that is. This is the healing of the unconscious memory wipe that occurred when you entered this plane as a baby. This is deep healing—a reconnection back to the Source of all.

The truth is, you were never disconnected. It was just the consciousness of that connection that went unconscious for a while. That's all. You have always been and always will be connected; you are just conscious of that connection now.

So, with that conscious connection, reconnecting your power and your truth, what truths do you embody, bring home, and step back into now? If you are so connected to everything, how do you harness that power and energy and channel it into your Life Purpose, into creating the life you truly want to live? To create what you're born to do?

You are the 'Black Sheep' of the family. You usually have to 'carry the family' somehow, even if you do not speak to or see your family anymore. You would've gone through deep grief and rejection of your blood family lineage. You have gone through and healed so much more than anyone else. You know it is a constant evolution and that there will always be 'something' that comes up, but you are getting savvy and catching it, transmuting it, and shifting it almost instantly. This is called emotional intelligence and spiritual maturity. You know there are times for deep-dive bouts of healing. Then there are times when it shifts almost instantly—with just a thought and a conscious understanding of what is going on. This is Mastery.

You've always been, and usually still are, the 'odd one out' in your family. You have always been somewhat estranged from family, even when you're right there with them. You have always been different from your family. You've even wondered how you've ended up with this family at times! You have always felt like an outsider in your family since you were little. You are also the healer and counsellor of the family, and most times, everyone comes to you at some point about something to heal or talk about. Or you have had dreams of a family member or two coming for consultations in your healing office!

You have either physically and energetically separated from your family system or know you need to. You have done a lot of generational lineage healing and clearing of the family line, or you know you need to. You know you're the karmic breaker for your family.

When you stepped outside the family system, you didn't even have a room to return to, so you left and never returned. You've always been on your own, and for whatever reason you originally left home, you have wandered whichever land you walked on ever since. It has taken a while to 'realise you are home' and finally find your grounding where you are. However, that is a huge inner journey in itself, and 'alone' here is a different 'belonging' alone.

You regularly feel like you don't have anyone because you literally don't. You don't know what it feels like to celebrate birthdays or other 'designated holidays' with family because you've been on your own for a long time. You have had offerings and invitations and gone to 'friends' places, but that family connection is different, and you don't know what that is. Even when you do celebrate it, you still feel it on the outside. You're probably wondering if that feeling *ever* goes away. I am here to tell you it does; you *can* heal from it. You can. And one day, you will.

Your Grandmother and/or Grandfather Is Your Everything. When going through your spiritual awakening, there is a huge connection, and part of your journey is that your grandmother or grandfather is very strong for you. This can be just for the first few years of your awakening or carry through your entire life. I will refer to Grandmother from hereon in; however, refer to this as who it was for you—be it your grandfather or an auntie that was like a 'Grandmother' to you.

Grandmother energy is/was the only 'lifeline' of complete unconditional love—someone who made you feel seen. When this is strong for you at whatever point in your life, you will be at the generational clearing lineage level of your spiritual awakening and healing. You are breaking the chain of negative influence in the family lineage (generational healing). The love remains; this love you feel from and for your grandmother will be what is 'healing and clearing' the lineage.

Grandmother Energy Healing also occurs when you tap into your Primordial Spirit and find who you are. This love that you felt and feel for your grandmother is what is tapping you back—it is the gateway, the doorway, the portal to your Primordial Spirit. It reminds you of your power, who you are, and the truth of who you are—you are loved, you are loved, and you become more loved. This is your natural essence; it keeps you connected to who you are. *This* is your Purpose.

More often than not, Ancient Blooded Healers never felt part of their family and, therefore, always became a lesser version of who they really were to try and fit in—to be loved and accepted. There are many who turn around and say, 'Oh no, I was loved and had a good upbringing.' And yet, more often than not, they are the ones who stay in less than satisfactory relationships, giving up their true desires to stay in the relationship, calling it 'compromise', which is what a relationship is all about.

We all know that doesn't work. One day you wake up from that relationship role, break the family system dynamic of being that role to them, and step into who you truly are. This is when Grandmother will become strong for you, reminding you of *who you really are*. Whether you are breaking away from the family system or you are breaking away from a relationship that is 'snapping the ties' to this pattern in the family lineage, Grandmother will be strong for you, as she is helping you through this portal, stepping you into you, not a replicated family system version of you.

Now, not everyone has kind Grandmothers, so it could be another person in your family system who played this 'role' for you, or it could be someone outside of your family. All it takes is one person to be that for you to break the relationship role, shift the karmic generational lineage, and heal so you can become your own person outside of the family system. Mostly, the 'new generation' has had more conscious parents than our history gone by (thankfully!), so it may be the mother or father who has this 'Love Role' that is so deeply connected to your heart for you.

It is also at this place that you bring Divine Balance to your Chakras. You heal the distortion in your Chakras and energetic body. The Masculine and Feminine come into Balance. You do not rely on outside sources to fill or nourish you. You don't seek validation from anyone and are not influenced or affected by Sources outside of you. It is here; you've grown up. You've become yourself, separate and outside of your family and societal system; this is where your true power lies. It's not that you don't interact with them, but the subconscious influence is not connected anymore; you've connected back to your true Source connection and creation. Manifestations and reality shifts accelerate here because you're not energetically plugged into the family or societal system of beliefs that have created your reality to date. With this shift, you feel more connected to life than you ever have before. In unplugging from inauthenticity, you've plugged into your own true Source of authenticity.

You've Become Sovereign

Books Are Gold To You. You have a ton of books on your shelf you haven't even read, don't feel called to, but won't let go of because you're 'energetically' reading them. The reason you won't let go of them is that your Ancient Blooded Healer lineage and gift allow you to absorb the content of the books. Just like sensing and picking up other people's energy, you also sense and pick up the energy of books and absorb them. You read them by absorbing them. Books will be the first thing you pack up if you move house. If there was ever a fire, you would run to your bookshelf first. You *love* finding old books and ancient texts, and you have a fine collection of them.

You're Somewhat Obsessed With Ancient. Okay, A LOT obsessed with Ancient Lineages, ancient ways, cleaning, clearing, ritual, and health and wellness techniques. Anything to do with the Old World and the natural way of living is normal and 'makes sense' to you. You love learning about the old generational lineages. You're obsessed with Dragons, Atlantis, Glastonbury, Avalon, and anything spiritual. You would walk around old villages, old cottages, old lands, and forests for days without even being conscious of time. You get upset when you have to leave places that are long-lost homes. You feel so connected; even hanging out in old cemeteries makes you feel most connected and at home.

You're at either end of the scale. You haven't travelled much, or you have travelled so much; regardless, you've walked every inch of this Land. You've always had a deep longing to travel, but you haven't travelled as much as you would've liked because it seems every time you go to do something, the Universe has other plans, and life has 'taken you' on a different path than what you 'planned' or 'thought'. If you have travelled so much, you wonder if anyone has truly travelled as much as you have, and it seems like not many you know have travelled near as much!

At the same time, you've lived a different life than many, walked a different path than most, and don't have a normal life either. You've travelled in such a way that you lead a very different life from 'normal mainstream society'. You rarely encounter an Ancient Blooded Healer with a white picket fence lifestyle (WPFL) (wait, do those even exist?). Or, you may have travelled a lot already in this lifetime and are deeply connected with the Lands and its people, activating a part of your Soul's Life Mission in a deep way that most don't understand.

You reach a point where you're ready to find your 'Home's Land' and settle for a time. Adventure always calls you, regardless of what 'stage' you are in the 'travel' department. I also find that those who don't travel often can find themselves entangled in a lot of drama and chaos or are more depressed than those who do. This is because you are someone who thrives on the stimulation of a new environment; you love being on fire in what you do and coming alive at the pace of getting shit done (in your own flow!). If you want to heal drama and chaos, tend to the part of you that desires travel and freedom. Pay attention to your inner Gypsy and watch your life and reality go from drama to thriving quickly. You may be deeply spiritual in your 'Home' and frequently travel to other realms via meditation if you are not physically travelling. Our Ancient Blooded Healer Souls are natural-born travellers of this reality and frequently converse in other realities.

When you are obsessed with a certain country for a particular period of time, it is because you are healing Past Life Wounds from that Land. You have walked that Land at some point before this lifetime, and it is deeply familiar to you. You may study the Land, be obsessed with its culture, can't get enough of watching a particular series about the Land, or even cook meals from that culture. That is because you lived on it at some point, and at this point of obsession, you are healing from what happened during that lifetime there. That Land may still be very active and alive for you because the realm is still literally 'open', and you are still 'living' it in a multi-dimensional realm. Healing work around either finishing this task or closing it off may be in order, especially if you feel disjointed in your current reality. You could also be activating the Ancient Blooded Healer Lineage from that lifetime, the roles you played, the gifts you held, and the Life Purpose you lived there. You will bring the knowledge and wisdom you birthed into this lifetime. You are activating the

DNA in your bloodline from what you used to do there and here—the memories, the wisdom, the gifts, the abundance, the love—all the things.

Closet Ancient Blooded Healers

There are definitely Ancient Blooded Healers who are married and have a 'white picket fence lifestyle', but it is also not the standard WPFL! They usually travel in caravans (or private jets!), don't have 'usual' jobs, and live extraordinary lifestyles. Most of the time, they don't practise or tell people publicly that they practise their spiritual gifts; they are closet Ancient Blooded Healers. Most of the time, they even hide it from their husband or wife or their closest relatives and friends. Sometimes these closet Ancient Blooded Healers do travel a lot, but they feel deeply amiss with something in their lives, and that is because their gifts are hidden in the closet. If they do not travel, they are usually riddled with a sickness of some kind or carry extra weight that they have 'learnt to live with'. Life is good for them, but there is something locked away. And that ends up being suffocating, no matter how 'free' they are in their travels or 'home' with loved ones.

The other type of closet Ancient Blooded Healer is the one who is in a relationship they don't want to be in, ignoring their intuition about leaving a long time ago, and has now 'become what it is' in a relationship. These are the ones who are quite physically or mentally sick or have very strong addictions. They will have some kind of illness, usually one that the doctors are at a loss to diagnose or find out what it is, or they just won't get better no matter what is tried and tested. That is because it isn't a doctor's or healer's magic that will help them. Only listening to their intuition about their relationship will help them. Only listening to their intuition about their true Life Path will help them. And that is something they are not willing to do. Or too scared to do. Or just comfy and 'happy with life'. But something is deeply amiss. It becomes 'all about the illness' when the true 'illness' is not listening to their intuition. It will heal them like a miracle, fast and instantly, the moment they begin moving in the direction their intuition leads them.

Then there are the ones who are with a narcissist and make all kinds of excuses for them. They will also be the ones obsessed with healing modalities; they have all the remedies, herbs, potions, and lotions and know a ton about them, but nothing works for them because they are not looking to the true cause, which is ignoring their intuition about the relationship they are in. They have exhausted all healing modalities because there is only so much inner work you can do before you MUST take physical action to change your life and 'get on the path'. No magical Merlin or Dragon in your meditation can take the physical action to change your reality. Only you can do that.

Then there are the ones who will jump from healer to healer, from doctor to doctor, from modality to modality, and from coach to coach because they do not want to take responsibility for their own lives and want someone to do it for them. This point refers to the 'victim' point I mentioned earlier in the Abandonment section. Perhaps they haven't found the right Healer they can trust. Or modality that resonates with their Soul. Perhaps they are not ready to heal. Perhaps they do not want to. It is okay not to want to take on these people as clients. It's okay for that person not to be ready to heal. Whose judgement is it anyway of what they or anyone else should be doing with any healing modality or how they live their life? It's not your responsibility to fix or heal everyone, as much as we know we can. The reality is that in this line of work, you won't be able to save everyone. It is your responsibility to know what type of client and avenue of work you will take on, the road you walk in your own life, as well as who, what, and how you want to facilitate your healing business. In my 'Trust Your Intuition to Become a Certified Intuitive Healer & Life Purpose Activator' course, I talk a lot about the different avenues and even know which one is for you.

Dark and traumatic pasts are normal. 99.9%, if not all, of Ancient Blooded Healers have had very dark and traumatic pasts. Many have had traumatic experiences that many will not even hear of in their lifetime, let alone comprehend what it takes to go through such an event and somehow come out the other side. Many have been in jail, let alone the ones who have grown up in abusive and toxic environments that many don't even think are abusive! Let's not forget about the traumatic accident that changed you or the health scare you almost didn't recover from!

Out of the many Ancient Blooded Healers who have walked such a dark and traumatic past, not many actually heal to the courage level of stepping out and transforming their pain into their Gift and Purpose in the world. Many try, but fewer continue to achieve the level of success they originally sought. Here, who you hang around matters; if you have 'normal friends and family' around you that constantly talk you out of doing something different (and good!) in your life, you will more than likely stop what you are pursuing and go and get a 'normal job'. There is nothing wrong with that, if that is what you want. But if you are truly here to transform your pain into your passion and share your gifts with the world, you will have to cut some ties, pay to be in high-level mentorship rooms for a time, and change the circle of people you hang around. It is just a fact. But you may not *want* to, and you may be happy where you are, and that's okay. But if you're not, and you *know* deep down you are here for *more*, then it is time to shift, baby! Your message, your past, and who you have become from your past are important. Never underestimate that. Your past is not shameful; it is here to inspire others to rise like you know they can and are meant to.

We have dark thoughts. It is in our nature. With what we have been through. With the disconnect and rejection we experience. How is one ever supposed to heal from something they know is an issue, but nothing can change the circumstances to support that? Deep. Huge. And at this point, it feels like no one will ever understand you; no one will ever get it, and even when they try, you reach a point where you realise no one ever will. Ouch is an understatement. Cue the most alone you've ever felt in your entire life—that feeling just doesn't go away.

With the level of DARK that we feel and travel, it is normal to us. Some act on it and never return, then cross to the other side and regret it because they are not some magical angel where suddenly everything is better, as we are led to believe. When we die, we carry the same level of consciousness that we achieved in our living state here. That is why they regret it. It's better to deal with it here, or you'll just be born into unconsciousness again and start all over again. I have worked with many mediumship clients where, in session, we are healing the person that left the Earth plane more than the person left living.

It is so important to remember that when we think negatively in life, we are processing a trauma that is surfacing. 99% of Ancient Blooded Healers are extra emotional. You've probably been called too emotional, too much, or too crazy, and people just up and leave for no reason; you've probably experienced it all. Your emotions are the reason you are so potent and powerful because, in a society that is trained to disassociate from their emotions, you are extra emotional simply because you haven't learnt to navigate your emotions or hone them yet. Or, the next layer of trauma is surfacing. That is okay!

Back to what is so important to remember: When we are in a 'Dark Wave', it is because a timeline convergence is occurring, meaning a trauma is surfacing. This means that your body, system, intellect, Soul, and Life Purpose Path cannot not only hold it down and bury it anymore but also that you do not need to carry it anymore. This 'Dark Wave' is heavily influenced by planetary line-ups and external factors in your current life. It can also be felt from carrying other people's emotions. While these are not to blame, the meaning of sharing them here is that you will be extra sensitive, extra emotional, and extra influenced during these times. This can give rise to negative and dark thoughts.

A powerful mantra that my mentor once shared with me and that I have shared with many clients in heavy trauma since, especially when they are in the midst of a Dark Wave, is that:

'It is just energy'.

You repeat it over and over and over and over.

It's just energy; it's just energy, it's just energy, it's just energy, it's just energy, it's just energy, it's just energy, it's just energy, it's just energy—over and over until you feel slight relief.

This mantra is powerful because it is also reality and the truth. When you hear it, your body relaxes, and so does your brain, which 'let's go' of the stronghold it has over you. While there may be deeper healing work to do here on the issue that has surfaced for you, sometimes this alone can shift it. However, knowing when to do deeper work and what to do with that is, of course, what I teach in-depth in Trust Your Intuition to Become a Certified Intuitive Healer and Life Purpose Activator. In short, if it keeps reoccurring, then it is definitely something to work deeper on with the right modalities, facilitator, and practitioner.

It is so important to understand that, as an Ancient Blooded Healer, you are so, so powerful. You are powerful at Healing others. You are powerful at creating your reality. You are different. You heal others by clearing and purging for them (hence why training as a professional Healer and getting paid for it as your career choice is highly recommended because you are doing this anyway, and let's not forget, most other careers leave you unsatisfied anyway! Your Soul thrives on this stuff! This is what you live for—what you were born for, right?).

To understand the energetics of what you are dealing with, with your own traumas surfacing on timeline convergences, feeling the emotions of people you are in contact with—feeling their subconscious stuff—the clients you work with, and other influences like chemicals in your environment and planetary line-ups, volcanoes shaking the Earth, modern-day stresses, relationship issues—phew! So much you pick up on! Why? Because you're an Ancient

Blooded Healer. You're One Of A Kind. You're a different species. You're so sensitive to your environment and the people in it.

It is so important to learn to hone your sensitivities. This is why I teach what I teach in Trust Your Intuition to Become a Certified Intuitive Healer & Life Purpose Activator and also speak deeply about it in my other books, because if you do not:

- Understand the energetics of what you are dealing with.
- Understand that it is 'just energy'.
- Know how to navigate the 'it's just energy'.
- Know how to navigate the dark thoughts.
- Understand how to ride them.
- Understand what they are teaching you.
- Understand that it is normal to be consumed by them and feel like you will never return from them.
- Learn to ride the waves.
- Knowing how to master this so it doesn't master you.
- Know how to take care of yourself in them.
- Understand the energetic components *while* you are in it and whether you need to cry, do a healing process from Trust Your Intuition or a different modality you resonate with, or understand if it is past life influencing, inter-dimensional influence, childhood memory, convergence timeline, or someone else's emotions you are carrying (which is not your job to heal, nor can you, by the way!).
It is a skill that is learnt and practised. It is essential to navigate your dark thoughts and know that this is a normal part of *healing*.

There is Nothing Wrong with You; You're a Different Species.

Learn how to navigate, understand yourself, and own the powerful gift of being an Ancient Blooded Healer. To be able to function in the modern-day world with so much clarity about all the energetic components that take us there and make us Ancient Blooded Healers in the first place, because this is exactly what is happening. Remember, it is a skill that takes practice; go easy on yourself. We navigate the Dark and the Light, but it is an important skill to learn because you're sensing it all anyway.

There is definitely nothing wrong with you. You have an extraordinary gift that allows you to see, understand, know, and feel the depths, threads, and distortions of energetic reality, ride them, heal them, and transform them back to the highest light to bring them all into balance.

Learning to navigate this will be your greatest attribute and skill, taking you to a different dimension of your own life. You will start owning your power instead of being floored by it and giving your power away to others by thinking there is something wrong with you, because there isn't.

One day, you will wake up and realise your power. You will have trained and honed your skills. One day you will reach a point where you will stop going to therapy and be very selective with the mentors you associate with and work with. You will seek out the ones who see your Ancient Blooded Healer Soul and the unique aspect of your gift within the Ancient Blooded Healer Lineage Lines.

One day you will deeply feel that there is nothing wrong with you; you're an Ancient Blooded Healer. This is where you start to own your intuition, your depth of knowing the realms; you travel without even trying; you multi-task in many realms and lands all at the same time; you heal yourself and others without even thinking about it—it is just so normal to you. You wonder how you didn't see this before, but now you do. It feels like you're free and can live your life now without needing validation or feeling like something is wrong with you. Ah, what a relief! You will get there one day, I promise. If you aren't already feeling this, you will. I believe in you, dear Ancient Blooded Healer.

You look younger than you are. You often get the, 'Oh, I thought you were a lot younger than that!' Or you get asked for ID at the strangest of places where you just shouldn't be getting asked for ID anymore. Even though you are slightly offended, you are also slightly grateful that they even asked you! It is common to look younger than you are, to have a fascination with staying as young as possible, to turn back the clock on your age, and to work on that consciously. You have frequently and often thought you would live until you're 130, 180, or longer. You've always been 'outside the box', but this is just a given for you. It's not something you think too much about; you just are.

You walk with thudding feet, and you also have a strong and loud voice. You have always walked heavily underfoot. People have even said this to you at times. 'Don't walk so heavy!' 'Why are you walking so loudly?' 'Why do you stomp when you walk?' And you look at them with a screwed-up face—what? This is normal for you. It may or may not have made you self-conscious over the years, but regardless, you walk with a heavy foot. You have a strong voice that you can project a long way. You have been called loud in the past, which may have made you dim your light to a capacity of some sort because you didn't even know or realise you were talking loudly—you were just talking!

At the same time, you also know there is deep power in your voice. You know you can project your voice a long way, have very strong energy when you talk, and can change a room just by speaking and using your voice in certain ways. Your voice can command attention when you want it, and you know how to use it. You love to chant, hum, or sing; you sing to plants, animals, and children; you have even looked at strengthening your vocal cords with lessons or other ways of using your voice over the years. You know your voice has a healing effect in some way, as many people have told you, but you also know that your voice is here to change the world in some way, shape, or form.

You're fascinated with Light and Sparkling, Shiny things. Whether through adulthood or your childhood (or both!), you have a love for shiny, sparkly things. You have a collection of shiny things, or you used to hide them from people. You are fascinated by the Light shining on reflections of windows, rainbows coming through crystals, or any sort of Light formation that catches your eye. The light shimmering on the water is something you look at for hours. You love sungazing, sunrises, and sunsets. You love all the light and dark contrasting pieces that make up our realm. You notice it; it stands out to you, and you frequently talk about it to people, or perhaps you have made a living out of it.

You have lived in or always had a fascination with Blue Houses—or the colour Blue in general. There is something soothing about Blue. They say that the ethers before we enter this realm have a blue hue to them, hence why Blue is very comforting for many people. You have always been around Blue. Or the paint peeled off the wall where you are living was blue underneath. You have lived in blue houses, or wanted to, or painted a wall blue, have blue bed sheets, or have a blue car—something fascinates you about the colour blue. Perhaps it is the ocean and its crystalline, healing waters of blue; either way, Blue is a thing.

You don't enjoy drinking cold water. Cold water isn't really a thing for you in the sense of drinking it. You enjoy cold showers, cold ice plunges, or cold ocean swims Wim Hoff style, but drinking ice-cold water isn't really something you would choose. You prefer room-temperature water and will frequently go out of your way to ask the store assistant if they have room-temperature water if you were to buy it.

Communication is eeevvvveeeerrrryyyyyyttttthhhhhiiiiinnnnngggggg to an Ancient Blooded Healer. You know the power of communication. You know that at the core of every issue is communication! And you know that communication solves everything! So, just communicate with me, and we will be fine! You can be riddled with anxiety if you do not have the communication you need in a situation, or you will be racking your brain trying to figure out how on earth they cannot see the fact that if they just communicated clearly, this would never have happened in the first place.

You see patterns in people. You're so clear about why and how someone behaves. Sometimes in the early days, to the detriment of your well-being. You'll make excuses, forgive, do the inner work, the past life work, all the things, but then one day, you'll snap, and the decision is made. You are highly clairvoyant and see patterns like clouds in the sky. You are super deep; you understand the intricate nature of all the dynamics, and that can be scary to others. It's just you being you. Don't stop that. However, your magic comes deeply into alignment with your Purpose when you learn to channel that into what you're being guided to do with it—a book? A video series? A YouTube channel? Something else? Start sharing your gift because it is exactly that—a gift—and people need to hear your message.

You cannot stand lying. This is like your pet peeve! You know the truth; you FEEL the truth; it is so glaringly obvious to you, so why do it? Seriously! There is no need to white lie, let alone be around people who lie, because, besides the fact that it confuses an Ancient Blooded Healer like you to no end, once you see it, you can't unsee it; it breaks trust, and that's that. Simple. You've learnt too many times to continue hanging around that, so yeah, you've chosen not to have those sorts of people around you, no matter the path you walk. When someone does not walk away from this realisation, they, too, go unconscious. Phew! Hello, society! Now you understand why you feel 'alone' at times and why you may not have many 'friends' because you would rather keep your circle small in deep honesty and integrity than be in mass confusion and unconsciousness, and that's okay!

You see the truth in everyone. You see the potential in everyone. However, holding that truth and everyone else to that standard can go against your own interests if you do not hold yourself to those standards. The potential you see in those for actual reality depends on where your own self-worth issues are. Living with someone's potential to step up is only a reflection of not owning your potential, feeling safe in who you really are, and stepping up to where you know you're meant to be.

You are waiting for them to step up because you're not stepping up. And even if they did step up, it wouldn't be satisfactory for you anyway, no matter how hard they tried, because this is about you, not them. You not 'being there yet' in your own potential will constantly have this inner nagging and unsatisfactory feeling because focusing on their potential is taking the focus off of you!

As soon as you focus on your truth, your values, and what is important to you and commit to that and not someone else's potential, that is when life really begins. This isn't about them. Your projection of them, their faults, or what they need to do will never satisfy you. You are the only one that can make you feel internally satisfied, and that comes from living your truth and purpose; that is when everyone else around you will 'satisfy' you. This isn't about them. Your potential is the only thing you are hiding from here; it is also your road map and lighthouse. Are you going to step into YOU, dear Ancient Blooded Healer? To YOUR potential and YOUR Life Purpose? To your Destiny?

You're not misunderstood; you're ahead of your time. And you're hanging around the wrong people. The reality is that no one will see your vision because it is yours! The only reason you're misunderstood is that it is your vision to bring to life; you're the only one who knows the intricate parts that pull it all together, so there is no use explaining it to people; just do the thing already. You're misunderstood because you're a Leader and meant to show them the way. You're misunderstood because you're hanging around the wrong people. It is so important for Ancient Blooded Intuitive Healers and Creative Entrepreneurs to be around their own kind; otherwise, you will simply forever be tied into the subconscious web of not only your family system but societal systematic dogmatic views influencing your life, no matter how much you say you're 'free' and out of that. The environment and who you hang around with matter. Period.

The Opposite Sex is Always Jealous That You Will Steal Their Partner. *cue rolls eyes and yawns* This one gets tiring, right?! Why does this always happen? You sense it almost immediately—they are threatened by you, and you haven't even done anything! You've just been being you, of course, and then some, and it can be so frustrating because you're just talking to them, just being yourself. Now. This is a deep one. I also know that you would've been on the other side of this, too; at times in your life, you would've been the jealous one or the fearful one. It is a thing. It is also a normal human emotion. How it plays out and where it goes from here depends on the person's level of awareness of themselves. What is going on at a deeper level is that there is a deep Soul resonance—a connection; it is a Soul recognition of who you are and who they are. And that is what they are feeling.

You know when you meet people and it's like you've known them for years? Or is there just something about them that just 'clicks'? You don't even feel sexually attracted to them; it isn't like that; it is just a deep resonance with them as a person. Not everyone feels this way with everyone, so of course, people can get jealous when there is this chemistry. And this is exactly it—it is chemistry. It can be so subtle.

On the other side of this, for example, if you are feeling jealous or like your partner is cheating on you and they truly aren't, they are genuinely committed to you, so you have no reason to be concerned, right? The reality is that you are a deeply sensitive, highly intuitive being, and what you can feel is this subtle shift in chemistry. Remember, honey, you feel the vibrations of the earthquakes in the neighbouring countries, right? *That* is how sensitive you are.

So when you sense your partner in this subtle chemistry Soul recognition interaction with someone else, it isn't that they are cheating on you; it is that you are feeling this because you are *that* sensitive. You can feel so deeply in the subconscious, in deep Soul recognition, that it does not mean they are cheating or going to leave you. If those feelings are over the top, of course, there is your own abandonment wounding to look deep into and heal. Just remember, you're sensitive, so, of course, you're going to feel a deep undertone of Soul recognition when two people meet—whether they are conscious of it or not, whether they are next door or on the other side of the world, *you* will feel it.

You can now see why it is so important for you to hone your skills with your sensitivities. Of course, jealousy to the extreme is your abandonment wound being triggered. That is a whole other conversation for another book and something to look at deeply and heal so that you can live without that constant anxiety and fear.

However, what we are speaking of here is that you feel these subtle vibrations, and it is so important for you to understand, hone, and realise what you are actually picking up and tapping into. This is why Ancient Blooded Healers can't stand lying because they are so acutely aware of the energetic interactions that are going on and feel them to their core. I'll say it again: fine-tune your skills, Ancient Blooded Healer!

Depending on your partner, if they are not as consciously aware as you are, they will be much less oblivious to these subtle vibrations, which is not something to even discuss; they simply won't get it. However, it is one of the biggest gifts you will ever receive as you fine-tune this level of subtle energetic threads and become acutely tuned into and aware of this level of energetic interaction. It makes you an extremely accurate and psychically powerful wisdom-holding Ancient Blooded Healer. You will be able to hold a level of space for people that is unheard of. It is just who you are.

The Witch Hunt Wound

When you are coming into your power as an Ancient Blooded Healer, when you're stepping out into the world and proclaiming who you are and opening up about your gifts, there is a societal stigma that is stuck in the consciousness of humans. This is the Witch Hunt Wound. It is especially strong in our blood, through our DNA, and is important to clear when you first step into this work. It will be the thing that is holding you back from stepping out in the first place or breaking through to your next level. My Healing From The

Witch Hunt's Wound Meditation deals directly with clearing, healing, and integrating this. This lock of consciousness about this Witch Hunt Wound is slowly being burned out of our collective consciousness and DNA as a whole; however, it is still there. You will find it surfacing any time you step out, especially at the beginning of your journey and at any level you are next elevating to. You can use the meditation each time to clear it any time it surfaces at any level you are stepping into.

Whether you step out or not, you may have felt ostracised from family and society, no matter where you are, who you are and have become, or where or what you do in the world and your life. This is a thread from the Witch Hunt Wound. It is also true that you are a different species, dear Ancient Blooded Healer.

You can do anything. You do all things at once and some. You are so conscious and right there with your entire creative mess, and you know exactly where it is; you know where all the pieces are; you can put it all together and some; you are extremely aware of all the pieces going on at the same time; and you are not sure how it is not this clear for everyone else that you see it like this. Honey, you are gifted; own it.

You will have had people in your life tell you that you are cursed. People will call you a witch, usually not to your face. How many times have you found out that people have spoken behind your back about you being a witch and even accused you of cursing them? **cues eye rolls and yawns** The only 'curse' is that you have this natural ability to bring people's subconscious to light for them. Their subconscious and buried emotions surface when you're around them or have been around them. *That* is a curse for them because they do not know what to do with the emotions they have buried and not felt.

Remember, society has been trained not to feel, and yet, the human race is a feeling sentient race, causing chaos and world mess due to humans not knowing how to use their natural abilities. My purpose here is to teach people how to feel and the intricate nature of understanding it. Feelings, emotions, and being clairsentient are just who we are. The ones who tend to project this 'You're a witch!' scenario most onto you are the ones who are the most closed-up emotionally. The lights are on, but no one is home, or they have a lot of Throat Chakra-related issues.

They may say you 'hold a heavy energy', 'that you are dark', cause trouble', or anything else along those lines. But they also, 99% of the time, can't stay away from you, will block you, delete you, stalk your page, and then want to befriend you. **yawn** These very same people will pretend to be your friends, be your friends, and then say things behind your back. It is only because you are triggering their subconscious. What a gift and what a ride, all at the same time!

These people are usually the ones who teach you a lot about boundaries, self-respect, and self-love, and you change your life because of them. Thank goodness for this; the intricate gift of the subconscious, the intricate gift of your intuition, is fine-tuned and honed by these people. At the time, it can be hurtful and confusing, and you may feel like you don't want to be on the planet anymore. Once processed, regaining your strength and confidence, fine-tuning your skills, and getting your life back, you are grateful to have gone through this, for it indeed did allow you to trust your intuition and understand it on a level you would not have before your experiences with them. There is a lot I can say on this subject of The Subconscious, so let's move on to our next chapter.

Chapter 3

The Subconscious Is So Clear To You

I went through a period in my life about 18 months after stepping into my online business when I was met with so much resistance from my family and the people closest to me. I had been doing this line of work since 2005, but it was in 2016 that I took it all online. I guess people living on the other side of the country could then 'see' it because it was all online and publicly available for all to see. Anyone who has an online business knows that this is normal. It's how an online, worldwide business runs—any business, for that matter, is public to some extent!

It was one of the hardest times of my life around that 18-month mark, and the most challenging part was that I couldn't figure out what was going on with my family. I knew I wasn't doing anything wrong. I was being my FULL self. I was happy. I had found my outlet in the world. I LOVED getting on videos and sharing my heart and soul—all of it—but they would shut me down. After several major events, I had the biggest 'aha' moment that would change the depth of my career forever.

Their subconscious is so clear to you; however, it is a skill to realise that what you are picking up energetically is not yours and then decipher it. To some, this comes naturally; to others, some fine-tuning of the skill is required, and for both, practise, practise, practise.

You are energetically picking up their subconscious stuff (which may come to you in the form of a mental or emotional state of mind and being), especially when you don't realise it. It is *why* you doubt *yourself*. It is why you turn away from your gift time and time again. I am here to help you hone your gift, step into your power, and free yourself and the world.

You pick up others' subconscious energy without realising it, which is why you don't trust your intuition. It's why you go around and around in circles, feel rejected easily, and feel like you've done something wrong most of the time. But you haven't done anything wrong. What you are feeling when you feel this is their judgement of you. That judgement is stuck in your aura as a thought. This is why it is imperative to learn how to clear your energetic field and do this on a daily basis. It will eventually become a way of being.

Most people judge us simply because they don't understand us. Even if they say they do but deep underneath they don't, we also feel that, and that is a lot of confusing energy going on in the space! They say one thing; their energy says another. If we are not clued in enough, we get confused by the head-heart difference, and then we end up feeling that confusion, and it is one great big energetic entanglement of a mess!

We are super sensitive; we pick up so many things; we are energetic beings; we just know things; we feel people's emotional buried baggage and emotions; we feel the Earth; we feel our neighbours and people on the other side of the world; we pick things up intuitively without us even being in the physical vicinity of them.

In my Trust Your Intuition to Become a Certified Intuitive Healer & Life Purpose Activator Course, I teach you how to fine-tune it, how to turn it up or down, how to tell if it is your energy or someone else's energy you're carrying or feeling, how to clear wounds, and how to step into joy so you're not subconsciously recreating your sad, traumatic reality over and over again with a negative wounded heart.

Let's say you're in a relationship, whether with a friend, partner, or family member—usually someone close to you at the start. As a sensitive intuitive, what happens is that we feel the other person's buried emotional pain. Let's say the person you're speaking with, you know, isn't as intuitive, spiritual, or conscious as you (not an ego thing, just reality). You know you have a gift, but the person you're speaking with doesn't have that same level of awareness.

You sense and pick up information about them intuitively; you don't try; it is just what naturally happens. What you're picking up is their subconscious reality; it is their unconscious 'baggage', the buried pain, the things they haven't dealt with; it is the 'dark' stuff, the things that they have swept under the carpet, turned a blind eye to—the things they are unconscious of.

Dark = simply unconscious. Not scary, not heavy, just unconscious.

It is the subconscious. They say the subconscious in someone is 90%, and the conscious is 10%. It is a lot. (Some say this percentage has changed in the last few years, and I agree, but let's use that example for now).

As an Ancient Blooded Healer, we sense their subconscious. That 90% is what we 'read'.

When I began this journey, I would be talking away, just talking away, you know, as we do—just speaking and being normal—having a conversation with someone.

What I didn't realise was that I was picking up and 'speaking' their subconscious stuff. Not in a derogatory way, but I am just intuitive; I would say, 'Oh, this is what I am feeling; this is what it is.' I didn't even think about it; it just came out so confidently. I was just saying what came to mind; I was conversing with a friend. You're just being yourself with a friend, as you do!

You're Being Real.

Then they fired up, had the biggest reaction, cracked the shits, and didn't speak to me again, and I was like, 'What just happened?' This would happen repeatedly in different scenarios for quite some time.

Some would then say, 'You're crazy; you're fucked in the head; what the fuck do you think you're thinking?' I would get ripped to shreds, and it fucking

HURT. Sure, there is a fine line between domestic violence and abuse, but that is a story for a whole other book, so let's stay focused here for a moment.

It took me a while to understand what was happening. This understanding and learning of the Subconscious and how much we, as Ancient Blooded Healers, pick up so naturally and truly understand in clarity about ours and anyone else's subconscious is the game changer for realising that people don't hate us. They are not rejecting me, but it deeply felt like it until I understood it, and still, today, I need to catch myself at times and realise this over again.

They don't hate us; they are not rejecting us. It is that we are picking up what is unconscious to them. We bring their darkness to light, their subconscious to consciousness. We do it without even trying. It is just who we are. It is why people—family and friends—don't like to hang out with me too much because I bring up too much for them, even without a discussion about any of it! My whole world changed when I began to understand this. Of course, I felt alone. Of course, I went through huge grief and even anger at times because of who I am. But at the same time, there was a sense of relief and freedom. They don't hate me, and my rejection wasn't personal; I am just someone who brings up all their unconscious stuff, and that is a lot to handle for people who:

- Don't know what to do with old pain and trauma that are buried in their subconscious.
- Are not ready to heal it, face it, or deal with it?
- Don't even realise that is 'why' or 'what' is coming up when I hang around them.

This is why you doubt yourself; it is why you hide; it is why you shy away; it is why you shut up and shut down your gift. It is why you turn away from life. You haven't done anything wrong; you are just picking up on what is unconscious to them.

When we are spoken to like this, sensitive Ancient Blooded Healers absorb it like a sponge—literally, we absorb it so readily because we are just being ourselves. We weren't even thinking about it; we were just talking away as you would with a friend or someone you care about. You just talk, right? Then, to have that thrown back in your face, we immediately go into thinking we have done something wrong. Once this 'wrongness' sets in, it opens the doorway for you to energetically carry all of their stuff. You are confused, trying to figure out what it was that you said or why that is even an issue because it is the truth and 'what it is'. So what is the issue? However, you have upset them, and you shrink back, don't usually speak much again, and hide your light and your happy-go-lucky self. You dim your light. You shut down.

The 'wrongness' that you are carrying is their energetic judgements about you. However, as much as we know this isn't true about what they say about us, we 'shrink, hide, and dim' because we don't want to upset them; we care about them! And we certainly didn't mean to make them upset. This is a potent sign that you've tapped into a truth that is still unconscious to them. You are here, reading this, because you're coming into awareness of *your gift*.

There is a difference between speaking your truth confidently and holding the line no matter someone's reaction. However, what I speak of here is when an Ancient Blooded Healer is coming into awareness of their gift, purpose, and the depth of energetic understanding that they sense and pick up naturally. You could say that we are closest to animals with the level of sensitivity, power, and potency of our gift.

The Clairsentient Sponge Clearing Activation/Meditation came through specifically for people like us when I channelled the Crown Chakra Consciousness Course. It is way more powerful than normal chakra clearing and is highly recommended if you feel that 'chakra clearing' doesn't do it for you anymore. It is a 'Sponge Clearing' for Ancient Blooded Healers, highly sensitive empaths, intuitives, and psychics—or anyone who needs clearing—especially after heavy situations, events, and conversations.

When you pick up on someone's subconscious reality and a reaction has happened, they will react differently depending on the person.

They will either:

- Never speak to you again.
- Go into a silent cave.
- Fire up, get angry, speak full of rage, and turn it around on you (this is usually because they are 'scared' of psychics even though they want to hang out with you and try and hide what you discovered—the truth—which is why they turn it around on you and gaslight you. This borders on abuse, depending on the situation, and is not okay, nor is it that you continue to hang around people like this, by the way.)
- Throw you under the bus.
- Contemplate how you knew that, but stay silent and change the subject.
- Contemplate how you knew that, ponder it, and then share that they realise you have made a very valid point, and they will look at it more.
- Contemplate how you knew that and sigh with relief that you helped them out and shifted what was going on and they didn't know.

Remember, you haven't done anything wrong.

You've Picked Up What is Unconscious to Them.

How they respond to that will depend on who they are as a person, their emotional intelligence level, and what they are ready for.

Understanding that I was picking up their subconscious was the biggest game changer in how I approach 'the real mainstream world', including family and friends, in holding myself in conversation, in becoming the listener instead of the talker, and in showing up in the world. I began to understand a whole new level of consciousness, let alone the intricate nature of my intuition, through this practise.

I wasn't hiding my light or changing who I was.

I was becoming the Walking Wisdom Holder rather than dispersing that energy to those who weren't ready to hear. What I did say became more potent and held more weight. I owned my power. I held a power that allowed me to transform a room, heal a person, and shift an entire collective consciousness without even saying a word. I could hold space for people I had not been able to hold before. I became more conscious. My vibration rose even higher. I was more aware of what threads I was picking up that were mine, deciphering what was in their subconscious and what was coming from Spirit, from consciousness itself, about the situation—all in a split second because that's how we Ancient Blooded Healers roll. If you've ever seen the movie Limitless (where he takes the pill to enhance/activate his visions), it was like that—being shown right in front of me (but in my Third Eye and all intuitive senses at the same time)—but it was deeper and more intricate than Limitless. When I watched that movie and the TV series (I was so engrossed with it at the time), I was like, 'No!' You don't need a pill for that shit! That is NORMAL! Goddamn, how they train society fumes me! Hence, I do what I do in the world! #rantover

When I went through this change, I became quiet. Very quiet. It was almost like I didn't want to talk anymore. All I did was talk online and talk to anyone who would listen about anything and everything. One could say I didn't have boundaries, and if I look back, perhaps I didn't in some respects. What I also recognised was that I wore my heart on my sleeve. But deep down underneath was the lack of love, validation, appreciation, and just simple care from my family lineage that I was still healing from. And that took time. Once this switch happened and I 'became quiet', it was the biggest reset and recalibration in my career, business structure, and personal life. Everything changed. I changed. And so did my entire world.

You Change The World, Just By Being Who You Are.

You're picking up that subconscious reality; you're so intuitive; it's normal; you just pick it up; and please, dear Ancient Blooded Healer, realise this mostly: you pick up way more than you're conscious of.

My wise mentor Lois once told me, '99.9% of the stuff you're feeling is not yours.' It was a massive eye-opener at the time, and ever since, it has helped me fine-tune this 'subconscious pick up', because it is so true and why it is so important for Ancient Blooded Healers to fine-tune their skills so you literally do not think you're crazy and check yourself into a mental ward—no, you're highly psychic, and you must learn how to hone this; it is your duty, your responsibility, and a huge part of your Purpose.

If you are not strong and clear in yourself, that is when you will think that you are wrong, doubt yourself, question what you said, and then agree with *them*, whether to their face or slowly hide away, when what you said was so true and right for you, it was so clear, and of course, it shone the light right in there, hence why you said it—you didn't even think about it. You just picked it up; of course, that is what is going on; it is second nature to you. And why didn't they see it like that? Why *don't* they see it like this? Honey, this is your Ancient Blooded Healer lineage; it is who you are. It is so normal to you, which is why you said it. It is why you feel different from everyone you know, except for a few other Ancient Blooded Healers you're starting to connect with now. That's why. It is just from here that you learn to fine-tune this skill.

When we are not conscious of this happening, it sinks us into a deep depression. Dimming your light and turning it off is cutting off your connection to the Source. Depression is pressing down on your Crown Chakra, pushing yourself down, rather than opening your connection to the Source that *naturally* streams through you. Our Crown Chakra is where this connection enters. It is why we are born 'crowning' into this world as babies—that is the connection to this world. Sadly, many babies do not get this experience today, and so it is a whole other ball game entering the world to deal with or tackle.

Addictions stem from this cutoff from the Source. We have addictions as coping mechanisms to 'feel happy', but it is fleeting happiness and not sustaining. We go up and down with our emotions like a yo-yo and are not always grounded. We are still highly psychic, intuitive, and connected; we are just not able to sustain that, let alone clarify what is going on, so we are constantly a mess with everyone's subconscious stuff intertwined with it all—yikes! No wonder we *do feel* like we are cray-cray at times!

As you start to realise your power to pick up their subconscious stuff naturally, it may switch overnight, but it is also a muscle. You become more conscious of it and may find yourself at the beginning 'still in the argument or disagreement' of what is going on. Then, in the moment, you catch yourself because you realise you have picked up their subconscious stuff and 'become it', so to speak. As soon as you catch this, you stop talking. You stop. You breathe and realise this. How you approach the current situation will depend on your partner or the person you are conversing with; however, you stop. You realise that it's not you. It is them; it is their subconscious you have just picked up, and you stop, with deep conscious awareness of what to do with this next step, rather than react. You're taking responsibility for how your subconscious interweaves with theirs and can separate the two. You've learnt how to 'be triggered, be conscious of it, shift, and hold space' all at the same time.

Yes, this is a skill; yes, this takes practise, practise, practise, so go easy on yourself in the beginning. You are learning your gift; you are understanding your subconscious and their subconscious on a different level. You are realising a deep truth about consciousness and how to navigate it consciously. This is a skill, deep in the Third Eye Chakra Consciousness, of understanding the dynamics of relationships, no matter 'who the relationship is with'. You are understanding your Clairvoyance on a deep, conscious level right now.

You have a highly analytical, extremely tapped-in Spirit Mind. You are so connected to Spirit that people often say you're off with the fairies, that you come out speaking 'out of this world' stuff, or that you often did so much as a child. You have a very powerful mind, and it can be our arch nemesis if we are not aware of this and purposefully train our minds. When we sense energy, what happens is that our Aura feels everything. This 'bubble of energy around you' is the first 'layer' that feels energy around you and that comes to you from the other side of the world, from cosmic energies, and of course, from people. You feel and sense everything.

For this example, I will assume that a person is thinking of you about a situation you both experienced that ended badly and has been left unresolved. Let's say that even though you feel resolved in the situation, the person feels abandoned by you, but you're not aware of this. You set boundaries, and it feels complete to you; hence, you get on with your life. Let's say five years have passed since the incident. This person is thinking about you, and all of a sudden, you start thinking of them, but you are busy in your life, whether tending to family or working, and so you brush it off; you don't give it much thought, but you did think about them for a moment too and got back to your busy life. Then later that day, you get home and start to relax, as you do after a busy day. Suddenly, you feel strange, like a strange, weird feeling. Then your partner gets home, and they've had a rough day, so they are in cave mode and need alone time. You feel concerned about this; you feel more abandoned by them than usual. You haven't been keeping up with your spiritual and energetic practises recently; you dropped them off a while ago for whatever reason after being so into them for a time. You try to connect with your partner, but they are more off than usual. This triggers you more than usual, and one thing leads to another, and you have a big fight, and you start feeling how let down you are with your partner and how they are handling the situation with you right now. Yikes! It all gets seemingly blown out of proportion, all while underneath, you have this nagging feeling that something isn't right.

You guessed it! That person you had the incident with five years ago who thought of you today that you also thought of briefly and then brushed it off or didn't think about it too much because, well, it was ages ago, it felt complete to you, and today you were busy working! That person's energy was now 'stuck in your aura' and playing out in your reality. No, this is not blaming the person from five years ago! Please stick with me while I explain these deep energetics.

This bubble of energy around you—your Aura—picks up all the energies. Perhaps this person was thinking about you; perhaps this person was in therapy working on healing from the situation; perhaps they were doing a ritual to release you; perhaps they were crying about the situation to heal from it. Regardless, your Aura felt it and 'sent the message to your mind' like an energy wave. Your mind 'noticed' it in your Aura, the first port of call to feeling this energy. Your mind sends out like a police radar force, 'What is this in the aura? In our energy?' Almost like a spider racing to see what has landed in its web because the subtle vibrations sent vibrations to the spider along its web lines, the 'thought energy from that person landed in your aura web', and the same thing happens: your mind 'tries to figure out what it is'. When you feel anything, your mind immediately goes to work to 'figure out what it is'. Consciously or subconsciously, we are doing this all the time. If you are not conscious of this, say because you're busy working and brush it off, your mind still works on this in the background because, 'Hey, there is a bug in our web!' If you are not conscious of it, if you don't travel it (as I call it), if you brush it off, your mind will still try and figure it out. When you are not conscious of this 'bug', your mind will pull up a similar experience from your memory bank that is similar in vibration and 'match' it to this. Yikes. What a mess already, right?

This 'little thought from the other person' sits in your Aura like a bug stuck in a spider's web. Now, the old emotions from the 'matched' event are starting to bubble up. But you're busy at work, so you didn't pay too much attention to it; you thought about it and forgot about it because you are busy. Because this is still sitting there, it is like a pebble being thrown into a pond; the energy of the 'entry point in your aura' ripples out over your entire aura. With its threads deep into the psyche of your mind and wherever you stored the original event in your body, this 'matched' energy memory also unlocks some buried unresolved feelings from back then, perhaps sadness that it ended the way it did, but you know it had to, and you had to set those boundaries. These buried feelings surface throughout the day, but you are busy, so it's easy to focus on the task at hand. Then you had space at home, and then with your partner getting home the way they did, this 'bug' stuck in your aura that has since 'rippled out over your aura' is now like a layer, like a cloud, like rose-coloured glasses if you may, that every event in your current reality is now clouded from. Not only is the energy 'from the outside' coming in and clouding your aura, but the buried event inside you and the 'matched' energy have also surfaced, so it is a triple whammy, if you will, the outside and the inside. Perhaps it wasn't a fight you got into. Perhaps it was food, alcohol, or some other addiction you sank into instead.

Now, there is so much we could dive into here that I am sure your mind has gone to—I hope it has! That is just one tiny event, one little thought from someone from the past. Imagine how every interaction on a daily basis has a layer of effect on you! Yikes! So, how about that energy clearing? How about that self-care? How about that exercise to keep your energy and body clean, clear, and strong? Of course, everyone will be affected differently, and I gave one teeny tiny example here. The threads and 'scenarios' that could possibly happen in a day at any given time and circumstance are limitless; however, this is an example to understand how much we are affected by energy, how much we can affect energy, and how important it is to train your very powerful mind to hone your psychic gifts. When you do, your spider's radar senses are sharpened. Instead of you brushing off that thought of someone from your past coming in and sticking in your aura (web), creating havoc in your current day reality, you are laser sharp and very clear in your energy, understanding what energy is coming in from where, what emotions are being stirred up from what, whether you just need to do a quick energy cleanse, or whether a deeper older trauma/emotion is coming up to be cleared out of your energy and body finally, therefore the deeper work you need to do. You become acutely aware. You become very conscious. Your psychic senses, intuition, and conscious awareness are amplified. You become a

Walking Transformer.

When you become aware of this subconscious dynamic and realise what is happening, it becomes conscious. It has become light. There is a time and place for deep healing, and there is a time and place when your consciousness shifts issues with your pure conscious awareness alone. You learn and hone the difference between needing to do a quick energy cleanse or sitting in meditation for a time to consciously check in with 'all your parts' (Shadow, Inner Child, Past Life, Deeper Trauma). You become acutely fine-tuned to the tools you need to use and when, whether that is requiring mentor help, a time and space carved out for yourself to work with them yourself, or chatting with your Inner Child and Shadow on your morning walk to gain clarity, healing, and release.

In these moments of realising the subconscious dynamics playing out, just stopping, breathing, and being present with it all can shift it by standing strong in your power, energy, and consciousness. By you becoming quiet, it shifts it. You are conscious of it, and your conscious presence transforms it. As you 'stop' and allow this conscious presence, you also allow the other person to come to the realisation themselves instead of telling them what it is. Remember, you're picking up what is buried in the unconscious, and when you 'witness' it by stopping and being in conscious presence to it (which is a skill, takes practise, and can be very uncomfortable in the silence), the 'buried' consciousness is surfacing, like a balloon that is held underwater or a bubble surfacing from the deep. Let it rise, because it is already on the way up. When you can hold space, witness this, and perhaps ask a question or two that allows the other person to come to the realisation themselves, true healing happens. A powerful healing happens. You didn't 'tell' them what it is; you held space for them to understand the buried emotion themselves by witnessing it, being conscious of it, and just allowing it to surface itself. You become a very powerful Healer when you master this skill.

As mentioned, every situation is different, and myriad scenarios can play out because no human is the same, nor is any trauma the same! Hence, I train my Healers at Reality Awareness to be Intuitive Healers because intuitive healing is paramount to truly allowing someone to be free of their past pain and live with the health and peace they seek. With practise and honing your skills, you will be able to differentiate what level of healing you need in any scenario. You will know if you are required to go deeper. This realisation can be like a lid on what has been buried and tucked away. All the emotions will begin flowing out. It might feel like it all happened yesterday, not ten years ago, but it is just time to heal it, that is all. All the old emotions should be coming out! You will feel like you're losing your mind. You will be howling in grief, wondering when it will ever stop! And it may not be at the most convenient time! However, you 'lifting the lid now' after 'all these years' is just you saving yourself from having cancer in another ten years, which is just this emotion festering deep in your body. So, go gentle on yourself and know when to reach out for mentor support from a trusted healer like myself or someone trained in this practise. This is what we do at Reality Awareness for this very reason.

Become the Master Cartographer of the Subconscious.

With these skills, you start to deeply hone your gift, understand yourself, and step out of the roles that have moulded you since childhood. People-pleaser roles, fawning roles, surrogate spouse and mentor roles, class clown roles, and other roles all start to dissipate when you come into your power. You begin to understand that there has been nothing wrong with you the entire time. You've been picking up their subconsciousness even as a child, and now you don't have to carry it, wear it, or think something is wrong with you. You're learning to separate yourself from it, decipher it, and know when to speak, when to hold back and hold space, when to walk away, and when to share your wisdom. You become acutely clear about it. You step out of taking responsibility for others and carrying their load and come into responsibility for your own subconscious intertwining and healing on a very core level.

You Come Into Your Power.

The only reason you drop into 'wrongness' and seem to wear it like an unconscious badge of honour is that, at one point, you DID speak up. You were voicing your needs, speaking the truth of the situation, and sharing it clearly and very concisely, and it was logical and common sense to you (doesn't everyone see it that way?). Remember, we always see things, feel things, know things, and hear things in the fastest, most economical way; it is just how we are built. We do things without thinking about them because we are so connected to flow, and our intuition is always on point. Remember, depending on the person, it will depend on how they react to you when you have spoken the truth. Over time, you hone your skills so that you know when and what to say, to whom, and how. Sometimes it is that you stop speaking 'to them' altogether and write a book about it instead, so the people who are ready for your wisdom and message will be reached.

However, if you're not strong or don't have the proper support around you, you give up. You gave up trying. You stopped asking for your needs to be met. You stopped worrying about shit that wasn't yours, and yet, you only cared about the situation, the item, or the event because it is in your nature to look after things and make things work smoothly so it doesn't all turn to shit.

There is nothing wrong with how you have handled this situation. What happens here is that eventually, you learn to let go of the things that are not your responsibility and do the best with what you have, and from this, you come into a greater level of embodiment of your true self with a powerful gift. When you do this, it frees up your energy from 'over-responsibility' for other people's issues and life events that have truly nothing to do with you (even when in the beginning you feel enormous guilt for not helping the way you used to) and allows you the space to realise your own life and channel your energy into your Life Purpose. Don't be alarmed if that doesn't become clear immediately when stepping out of roles of over-responsibility or any sort of life direction change and learning to do your own life for perhaps the first time in your life. It can be a good 18 months of recalibration, so go easy on yourself through this change. Remember,

You're Not Lost; You're Recalibrating.

Important points to remember that will keep you entangled in others' subconscious stuff longer:

- If you are low on self-care due to a major life change.
- If something has knocked you down recently.
- If you have let self-care slip just because.
- If you're using drugs, alcohol or another substance more than you usually do.
- If you're tired, worn out, haven't slept much, or haven't been taking care of yourself like you usually would.
- If you've been through something big in your life that you haven't dealt with or are still dealing with.
- If a major trauma is surfacing due to a timeline point.
- If your nervous system is on overdrive because of the above-mentioned.
- You can function in society really well, but something is bubbling up, and you suddenly don't feel good.

You will not have space to hold anyone, let alone yourself. Or you will for some time, and then that ball drops. You get tired, burnt out, want to walk away from it all, resent anything, anyone, and everything, and just can't shift out of your funky mood.

The solution? Self is a priority over everything. Something else my mentor Lois so wisely told me was, 'Self as a Priority, Others as a Necessity'. We make sure our self-care, energetic, and physical boundaries—everything—are always up to scratch as a *priority*. Energetic and physical health are necessary if we are to stay conscious of what is ours and someone else's. Deeper than this, it is clearing our own subconscious wounds to shift our reality to a higher vibration and attract completely different life experiences at the same time. I teach this in Trust Your Intuition to Become a Certified Intuitive Healer and Life Purpose Activator: the Clearing of Deep Subconscious Wounds.

Not only that, when you are low, you will be triggered a lot more easily, but the energetic entanglement is greatly deepened; you take on more of their subconscious or any negative energy floating around, and you feel worse. You become a magnet for it. This is where 'empaths' have gained a negative wrap in the spiritual community, or those 'looking into the spiritual' community, saying that they are heavy and clouded and all kinds of harsh things that only send people like us down further instead of helping them up. Remember, these people don't get it or the depth that an Ancient Blooded Healer feels; they don't understand our species.

Clearing your energy daily with chakra clearing or other energetic clearing techniques that work for you, *along with* physical body health, fitness, sustaining nutrition, and living in alignment with your values, is essential for staying clear of other people's subconscious stuff. Imperative even.

The next phase is sharpening and acutely learning your intuitive skills so that you are conscious of what energy is entangled, flying around, and deeply embedded in the current situation, childhood, cellular coding, nature, galactic, solar, and cosmic energies, past lives, and energetic coding. This is also what I teach in Trust Your Intuition to Become a Certified Intuitive Healer and Life Purpose Activator.

There are many ways and modalities that can take you into deep healing of your subconscious. *Some ways to get clear and hone your subconscious:*

- Healthy physical body (this is what houses your entire Soul; keep your sacred vessel clean and welcoming for your Soul. When you are grounded in your body, it is easier to understand your subconscious when you train your intuitive skills.)
- Heal Your Own Wounds
- Shadow Work, Shadow Work, Shadow Work!
- Inner Child Healing & Consistent Inner Work
- Personal Development
- Meditation
- Art Therapy
- Yoga
- Physical fitness and detoxing your body
- Joy
- Spending time with people, like truly present time with people
- Working with clients
- Trust Your Intuition to Become a Certified Intuitive Healer & Life Purpose Activator Course

Reading the Subconscious Is a Gift.

You are gifted. You are talented, and do not let anyone else tell you otherwise. Period. It is also normal for you. Remember, it is not normal for 'them', and that is okay. They don't get it. Maybe one day they will or won't, but for now, it is not your responsibility or concern whether they do or not. You can now move forward, mastering your reality, with the deep understanding that this is who you are, what you do, and that this is natural to you.

Your outlet for how you truly show up in the world—to share your gift and become who you were born to be—is coming. If you are already 'here with what you do', your next level is about to skyrocket!

Chapter 4

Wisdom Walkers

Ancient Blooded Healers are the Wisdom Walkers or Walking Wisdom Holders. We learn through experience. We can read something, understand it, and be told something, but until we do it and live through it, we can't really grasp it. When we live through it, this is a huge part of our Purpose—to share the Wisdom we have walked through. Ancient Blooded Healers' Purpose is to teach what they have walked through, what they have learnt, understood, and are usually now Masters at.

You can hold space for those who have been through what you have been through, and the common thread I have found is that you will always be able to help someone with something you have just shifted through in your life. Whether you're officially trained in it or not, you will have the understanding, compassion, and capability to coach someone through it. Not only because you've just shifted through it but because it becomes common sense and gives you a deep understanding of the intricate details that can only be understood by living through it. It is what shifts it for this person that the Universe 'just happened' to send your way so that you can help them. No matter if you have 15 master's degrees, your next client will always be something you've just lived through, not what you read in a textbook.

You would've heard floating around the Spiritual Community, 'The biggest Lightworkers on the planet have gone through the darkest past'. Honey, you are definitely a

Wisdom Walker.

You shift reality as you move through it. You create reality beneath your feet. Everything you touch turns to gold, and you can create anything you want to. However, touching it to transform it into gold can seem like everything falls apart, like you are a walking mess, and that you destroy everything you touch. People have probably even told you that in the past, just to hurt you some more. The reality is that nothing can be built on old crud. You can't come in and renovate a building or build a new one without destroying the old one first. You can't build a beautiful relationship without destroying old patterns and belief systems. You must conjoin and build a beautiful one based on mutual values and the relationship's definition of love.

You may have been told that you destroy everything. You may still be holding judgements about yourself, saying that you create havoc, change, and walk in and make everything a mess. Remember, when you bring up the truth of a situation, you bring up the unconscious. The unconscious *is* a mess. It *is* chaotic. It is not orderly and neat. You are a powerful Being of Light, and that Light is consciousness, and that consciousness is taken to the darkest recesses of people's minds simply because you exist. It is here that the most light can be held and shine the brightest. You do this without even thinking. It is a normal part of your Being. As discussed before, as you realise this truth about yourself, you also learn how to be the Walking Wisdom Holder. It is a skill, and you get better at this muscle the more you exercise it.

You can transform darkness into light, depression into hope, tears into laughter, and night into day. You bring light to everyone around you, and you're the one they remember when they think back through their lives and how certain people changed them.

Walking Wisdom Holders have learnt how to hold space for people. We become wise beyond our years. When we learn our gift, we screw our faces up in confusion when people say that we are wise beyond our years. This is just normal, isn't it? We don't see ourselves as different. But as life goes on, we experience unpleasant things that wake us up to who we really are, and it becomes a whole new experience of Being.

You've Become Embodied.

We learn how to hold space through experience. Holding space means you are conscious of something someone else is unconscious of. You have learnt, through experience, that not everyone is ready to hear the truth buried in their unconscious that you've become conscious of. Holding space is definitely a skill we acquire through becoming conscious of the depth of our gift.

I can see it clearly through different stages of awakening:

- Fighting/arguing, continuing to try and explain yourself and the truth to someone.
- Realising that they don't get it and never will, no matter how much you try to explain it. This could be explained as the 'giving up' phase. You can go 'silent' here, which isn't always a bad thing. You're just learning a different phase of the truth that is so clear to you that others are not ready to hear. You can be deeply triggered and want to say 50 thousand things, but you bite your tongue because you know they won't understand it and they 'need the last word' to feel in control. This is only because the truth in their subconscious is starting to surface, which is 'uncontrollable' because it brings about change, which is scary for people. Humans are creatures of habit. You can also be triggered here, but you're holding space for your own trigger, your own truth about the situation that is surfacing, and 'hitting up' against theirs while knowing what is surfacing for them. You're not 'feeding into it'; you're conscious of what is surfacing and allowing all to be pure consciousness. This is Shadow Work in real-time.
- You understand that just holding this conscious awareness of 'what is' allows them to come into their own realisation of what is bubbling up for them rather than you 'telling them'. Even though you clearly know what is going on, you allow it to surface for them. You can see and notice when they realise the truth because you

also see this shift. Whether right there and then or later on at some point in their lives.
- You are conscious that if a situation triggered your buried stuff to the surface, even though you held space for it, you did your own inner work afterwards to shift it for yourself. This integrates your shadow; this returns you to wholeness. This stops you from attracting the same type of situation time and time again. It heals the pattern. This is taking Responsibility as a Lightworker. Responsibility is Divine Step #8 in the 12 Divine Steps to Awakening Your Life Purpose.

Shadow Work, whether in meditation, real-time, or both, is the

Epitome Of Evolutionary Consciousness.

Feeling your feelings consciously brings light to the dark. Feeling feelings consciously is how we heal. You can be fully immersed in your feelings, howling on the kitchen floor in a ball of grief, unable to take another breath, and still be conscious of what is going on with your emotions. You can understand where they are coming from, the past life experiences they are connected to, the generational threads they are a part of that relate to when you were a child at five, and how that plays out in your current reality. This level of conscious understanding is built over time. As a gifted Ancient Blooded Healer, it's crucial to trust yourself when you have this level of clarity about how all these threads connect. When you are 'in it', you are healing it because you are conscious of it rather than having it unconsciously buried within you. The healing process won't be comfortable, feel good, or be nice. Healing is messy, raw, and uncomfortable as hell. Birthing a new reality is also messy, just like birthing a baby. Be okay with the mess because you are birthing a new you.

When you have walked the depths of emotions for yourself, you have this clarity of skill set in understanding consciousness, emotions, feelings, your intuition, and the subconscious, which is why you become so clear in your everyday life without needing to take ten plant ceremonies only to have to go back to the ceremony to understand it all over again.

No.

This is normal for you.

Own it.

You're An Ancient Blooded Healer,

This Is Your True Nature.

You Are A Wisdom Walker.

You can fine-tune these skills, for sure. Just like I speak of how we can all learn to drive a car, but if you want to become a rally car or grand prix driver, that takes extra skills, dedication, training, and fitness levels. The same goes for honing your intuitive skills as an Ancient Blooded Healer. It is easy for people to understand their intuition, but if you want to become a Master in your field, you must train and practise daily. It becomes a lifestyle.

It can be a very challenging time in your life when you come to a deep understanding of your gift as an Ancient Blooded Healer. Not only are you navigating the subconscious, but you also realise just how much you truly pick up on and how often you were correct, despite being told that something was wrong with you and that you needed help.

You are also learning about boundaries, such as who, what, and where to speak. It can be overwhelming when you awaken to all of this, usually all at once. It may be the hardest and darkest time of your life, and you may feel the most alone and on the outskirts. Despite your attempts to fit in, you always end up in the same place. However, understand that you are going through an initiation to understand your Life Purpose at a deeper level. You will get through this. It is important to surround yourself with others who are also walking this path, gain mentor support, and expedite your skills so you don't remain lost and wandering around, thinking that there is

It's harder when we're going through this alone. Even with a mentor's support, it can still feel like we're on our own. Even when we've found a beautiful Soul tribe online or in person, it can still feel isolating. During these times, it's important to be gentle with ourselves and know it's just a phase. This phase will pass, but it's accentuated when we haven't fully explored and healed our family lineage, abandonment, rejection, and betrayal wounds. As the black sheep of the family, we often take the blame for everyone else's issues while we're dying inside, and we feel like no one cares. We frequently think that the world would be better off without us, and there's no way out of feeling this way.

You're Not Alone In This Feeling

Even though it definitely feels like it at the time.

I'm here to tell you there is a way out, but it's not an easy path. It takes about three years to get through this feeling from when the original event that triggered all of this happened. Now, it seems like, 'Such a long time, Hannah; why did you just tell me that?' I am telling you the truth so that in 6 months, when another peak wave of it surfaces again, and you feel like shit all over again, you don't go thinking downward-spiralling thoughts all over again. This time, you will know another layer is releasing from you, and it is just what it is: another layer. The timeline points of the waves of emotions that surface like it was yesterday all over again are real. It is so important to understand that it isn't that you:

- Haven't dealt with it.
- Haven't healed it.
- There is definitely something wrong with you (no, there isn't! I *will keep* saying it).

- That maybe everyone is right (no, they are *not*).
- It feels like a deep, big black hole you can't get out of or even breathe in again, and you wonder, 'WTF just happened again?' (You *will* surface; please have faith in me when I tell you that you *will* get through this.)

Another wave is surfacing. That is all. We Wisdom Walkers have become adept at learning.

To Ride The Waves Like a Pro Surfer

And like my dear client said, 'Keeping her arms inside the cart and trying not to reach out and grab on, but letting go!'

It's like that. A roller coaster. A tidal wave. Or three—all at once, with a tornado thunderstorm in the mix—all rolled into one. And it feels like it will never end. But it does.

This is the nature of change. This is what happens when you create new systems and new ways of Being. When a big life change happens, everything collapses and falls apart, and do you know what else always happens?

You Get Through It.

Once you understand that nothing is wrong with you and hasn't been all along and that you have this deep, powerful, intuitively highly tapped-in skill, you start to stand up taller, you start to find a way to take care of yourself again in ways you didn't or have never had before, you start to find your confidence again, and even a smile starts to come out.

You're Clearer About Your Gift Than Ever Before.

But it takes time. And walking through the mud in the dark, all alone and some. I won't lie about that. I am good for the truth.

This is your initiation into your Wisdom Walking Role. And you will learn this time and time again at different phases of your life. And each time? It isn't that it gets a little easier, although it does, because you're not beating yourself up, thinking something is wrong with you. Even though it feels like something is wrong, you have learnt to understand what is happening and that this is another wave of release you are walking through—this initiation with conscious awareness—even though you are still feeling *all* the feelings. This is what Ancient Blooded Healers do.

You are the Wisdom Holder of the Dark and the Light.

We hold the extremes.

I remember doing a fast once and speaking to someone who didn't get it. I told them what I was doing, and her one comment shook me, and I caved. I look back on that moment and realise how much I did listen to her. A lot of it shaped my life, and at the same time, it was very traumatising. 'Oh, that's a bit extreme'. She said this in response to my cleansing and fasting. BUT I AM THE EXTREME!

I am the Dark and Light; I have it as my car number plate, for goodness sake! I sit there until it's finished; don't interrupt me, and this is how it is done! This is who we are: immersion learning and creative waves. It is a thing! That was one of those relationships in which I learnt (the hard way!) not to speak to people about what you are doing in your life if they do not understand. They just don't get it and will be the fastest ones to tell you not to do it, that you can't, and don't be ridiculous all at the same time. Ouch. It shuts you down; you start to forget who you are and what you value, and your quality of life fades away. The light has gone out.

Private Mentorship Changed My Life

Stepping into private mentorship with a high-level mentor in her mastermind for three years was one of the most powerful ways I stepped out of 'my normal surroundings'. I learnt many lessons from that mentorship, but it also broke me out of only having friends and family around me. Unless they are multi-millionaire intuitive Ancient Blooded Healer entrepreneurs and you want to step into intuitive entrepreneurship, you'd best be finding those who have led the way in such a field, not those who haven't.

Who You Hang Around Matters.

It took me a little while to understand this. It took me experiencing many different groups of people—families, friends, acquaintances, masterminds—to realise that they all strongly affect your life.

Hang around people who are heavily into drugs and partying every weekend; you'll still be doing it when you're 50, and hey, there's nothing wrong with that if that is what you love and want to do for the rest of your life. I was a hard-core raver and heavy recreational drug user from 17 to 21, and I had my spiritual awakening when I was 21, which took me off the drugs. Stepping away from this group took a few years in total, but when I stopped taking drugs, I realised it was the only thing in common with them, and finding new friends was a journey in itself. They thought it strange that I began this spiritual stuff full-time, and then when I had my daughter four years later, it was next level to them, and I barely spoke to any of them after that. When they began having kids years later, I think they had more respect for me, realising what it takes and that I was doing it on my own, unlike most of them as couples.

Hang around with heart-centred multi-millionaires impacting the world, and you'll get mighty uncomfortable as you step into new ways of being. Still, your life will get better, and you'll probably make some money, too—if you're willing to learn from them, of course!

To be honest, I struggled being in a room (mastermind) with people earning more than me and doing big things in the world, and yet, that is all I wanted to do. I shrank and stepped out of it. I regretted stepping out of it, but perhaps I had to learn the difference. Because

Who You Hang Around Matters

I had to come back to myself and heal my family's wounds. I was approaching the 17- to 20-year mark of living on the other side of the country from my family. While I had done a lot of healing work on my family lineage during all the years I had been away from them, stepping into my online business took it to another level and knocked me off balance. When I reached the 20-year mark of living away from my family on my 38th birthday, it was one of the hardest experiences I had ever faced. I was alone and still healing from the dog attack and the underlying trauma of my family's estrangement, all at the same time. However, I realised what that mastermind truly did for my life, and today I wouldn't be where I am without it. It brought my dreams to fruition, rather than remaining just a dream.

I was able to have concrete steps to bring it to life and be surrounded by others where this was normal, not weird or strange, or be told to get a normal job and stop doing this psychic shit. Trigger and challenge me? Oooh, yes, you bet it did. But it made my dreams a reality, rather than just talking about them. And it was essential to my growth in understanding business, running a company, working online and travelling at the same time, let alone what and how to have clients, how to deal with fallouts, and all the business, legality, and company essentials of stepping into the role of CEO instead of self-employed and genuinely owning your gift in a way that serves the world. My family and friends couldn't have taught me that.

Who You Hang Around Matters.

The reason you won't be happy going against what feels right for you is not only because it doesn't feel right but also because it goes against your values. For example, if you have just begun a new health regime and then meet a partner who ridicules you, laughs at you, or mocks you because you eat 'this healthy stuff', if you don't walk away from them and 'put up with it' because the sex is good and they are 'kind to you', you carry a layer of shame that is like a cloud and a cloak to your Soul, and you dim your light just enough to stay in acceptance of them, so you don't lose them.

This erodes your self-worth, self-esteem, and happiness. These seemingly insignificant remarks (which they will probably tell you are such and to 'get over it') sit on you, soak in your aura, and eat away at your Soul. Eventually, it is like a parasite, worm, or itch that has eaten away and reaches a layer where you no longer eat healthily. You eat what they eat and become a shadow version of yourself to fit in. This is not a healthy relationship. Over time, you will become resentful, put on weight, get sick, be unhappy most of the time, develop rashes, and feel exhausted and short-tempered. All kinds of things will mirror this reality you have let yourself stay in because you know your heart and Soul are screaming that it is *not okay*.

If you were clear on your values and that a healthy lifestyle is important to you—which it is—but also a non-negotiable in how you live your life and who you have around you in your close vicinity all the time, you would shine because you are living in accordance with what is important to you. For me, it was a huge learning and stumbling block for years, as I wondered what my values even were. I was just living my life and doing my thing, and I LOVED it, but then when people came along and ridiculed, laughed at, or told me to stop because it was 'extreme', simply because they didn't understand it, had not done the research, or cared to, it crippled me. I share some big, hard lessons with you so you don't have to walk through what I did and can fast-track your dreams!

It is okay to go through the darkest, hardest pains, trauma, and experiences of your life because you get through them and can help others on the other side, but you need to heal from them. If you are still talking about the incident that made you fall down a big black hole, honey, you're still there. If that is all you talk about to anyone who will listen, it is all you write about on social media and all you speak about to anyone who stops you in the street. You wonder why your friends don't talk to you anymore and why people look at you strangely, or you get strange comments from people that upset you all over again, and you're left sitting there in it. Because, honey, *you're still in it*.

It's Time To Heal.

What I hate the most is when people call others 'victims' simply because they always talk about their struggles. They are not victims; they simply haven't healed from the situation yet, and those are two very different things! If you know me, you know I hate the word 'victim'. The truth is, these individuals just haven't found the right Healer that can help them get through and past their pain, but the key is that they have to want to. They can say they want to, but they find all the excuses for why they can't afford it or won't do what is required to get them out of it. While some people would say, 'Yep, Hannah, see, they like their victim story!' I don't believe that is the case.

Deep down, there is a need that has not been met. They never received the nurturing, care, and motherly love they needed as children. They grew up in emotionally empty situations and relationships and always felt on the fringes. They dropped everything for everyone and never had anyone there for them. No one has ever had their backs. They have been thrown under the bus more times than they care to remember. They give everything and never get anything back, which has become a deeply ingrained belief. The huge, gaping hole they feel all the time builds resentment, and they know they are being used, but they still go along with it, seething underneath. The pressure builds up and up, and they usually end up hating their lives, but they won't change them. This is often because they don't know how to change, and that's where a trained healer comes in. They feel deeply stuck where they are and full of anxiety when they have to go to work. They are stuck in the role of serving everyone else and won't take care of themselves. One day, they may snap out of it or fall into a deep hole of depression because they don't know what else to do.

The belief here is that if I help other people enough, they will see how much I do for them and help me back. But does that really happen? So the next level is that they get sick, so they *have* to have people care for them to meet that need. It works, but is that really what they want when they get sick? To be sick so that people have to pay attention to them? This is why people stay sick because they don't know how to get this need met any other way, and it becomes this vicious, fulfilling cycle. They need to understand what is going on beneath the surface before they can start doing something about it.

People Don't Know How,
That Is What Keeps Them Stuck.

People keep talking about their 'victim story' until someone takes notice, which usually doesn't happen. Usually, they lose more friends and family than they had before. They drop deeper into addictions and hide them away, making them feel worse and go deeper into the big black hole than before.

They are not victims who choose to stay in their victim story consciously. They simply haven't healed. *But* the only *but* is that they have to *want* to heal.

And that?

That takes a willingness, a readiness, and a realisation that no one is coming to save me, to be here for me, to listen to me, to do anything, or even to care.

And that?

That is a big, deep, dark hole—the worst feeling in the world. To face that level of reality is gut-wrenching and creates the deepest grief in the world that one could possibly feel. Of course, avoidance is better. (Well, it is not, but to face that level of pain alone is just... OMG, don't go there, Hannah!) To grieve someone when they have died is one thing, but to grieve the reality that you have no one when they are still alive? There is a nothingness to that that is worse than death. Wait, how would we even know what death is like? Anyway, you get my point. There is a nothingness that is so scary.

But this feeling? Is one, only

Ancient Blooded Healers Walk.

When I point out the truth about how someone is not healing, I am told I am victim-blaming too. It is a fine line to walk, yet when we point out the truth buried in the subconscious and people don't understand that, they could see it as victim blaming. On Australia Day in 2023, I got agitated at people apologising to the Original Landowners. I was more agitated because I felt obligated to acknowledge them. I was frustrated about that because I am pissed off that they sit there and abuse us, white fellas, for something that was done 2–3 generations ago, and they are still blaming us for it.

Let's be clear about this: I do not support genocide and deeply respect what happened. I even have a course called 'Heal The Land' that teaches mediumship and land and earth healing. I created this course as I did a huge land healing back in 2017, helping souls with the genocide on this very land I walk on on the Sunshine Coast, Queensland, Australia. I have a lot of respect for and care for their pain. I know what it feels like to be scapegoated and an outcast!

But I was shown a different side—reality, if you will—of their situation in 2020 when I was road-tripping down to Victoria, Australia. I was blessed enough to have even gone to one of their settlements. I felt honoured, and you could sense the depth of the energy when you walked through the aura of the place. And yet, I was deeply disheartened and couldn't believe what I saw and heard. After a bit, we all took our places in their tent, and out came the bong, and it began. (I haven't smoked weed since 2006, but I sat there watching and listening.) All these plans to storm down Parliament, take back Australia, and take over all those buildings. The swearing at each other, the anger that rose, yelling at each other about what 'they did to us' and how we were going to get back at them, etc., and then waves of quiet as the weed kicked in, I guess. And I was like, 'What?' Sitting around smoking bongs on a Sunday afternoon, and then nothing changes, and we just keep blaming?

I left their eyes wide open. To say I understand their particular pain is a lie, but I do know what it feels like to be scapegoated and outcast from the tribe ten million times over. And I also know that trying to make someone see what they did to hurt you is like drawing blood out of a stone. Trying to wake someone up to see what their ancestors did is even more of a waste of time than sitting around smoking bongs, yelling at each other about what they will do to current-day people, and then packing another bong. Someone, please explain to me how that is changing circumstances.

This is what I wrote in my post on social media on Australia Day in 2023:

'I see you, Traditional Owners of Our Land. I honour you, pay tribute to you, and deeply respect what and who you are here. I am so, so sorry for all you have endured.

Healing your own internal trauma about what happened to your collective will shift mountains and create waves of immediate change.

Until that time comes, I hold space for your hearts hurt too. I see how angry you are and that you aren't ready to face that to heal it, so I'll hold it with you until you do.

#australiaday

I don't support genocide, but I don't support hurling blame and anger when internal hurts are not willing to be healed.

It's not about what's happened, but what we do about it.

No, genocide is far from okay.

But hurling abuse and anger without healing your own and collective hurts is also not okay.

I see you, and I hold space for it all.

I also speak reality and won't shy away from the deeper truths we all face today.

Peace on Earth begins within.

I got a lot of kickbacks for my post about it, as well as a lot of praise for speaking the truth. The issues that we face in Australia, which I am sure are similar in other countries around the world, will not be fixed by more alcohol bans and more police. We know that what is required is healing. Taking away the addiction won't solve the pain. The addiction is covering up the pain. The addiction is not the issue. The trauma is. But hurling abuse at white people will not heal your trauma. Only you can do that.

But here is the key: those people have to *want* to heal. And that goes for *anyone* in trauma. They might say they want to, but nothing changes for a long time.

And until that time comes, we just hold space.

There is a time for listening to people's pain and trauma. Then, there is a time for setting loving limits (boundaries) and speaking some hard, cold truths to rattle the cages of the continued painful stories and face them rather than talk about them.

Facing it = feeling it in the heart.

That level of grief in the heart—not talking about it and blaming others with continued anger—hides a huge level of grief that society is taught to avoid and cover up with addictions rather than face and feel to heal. That is what I am here to teach: to consciously feel to heal. Any substance, whether medicinal or healing, is still a cover for the truth of feeling the depths of the heart. This conscious feeling breeds emotional intelligence, our natural state of Being. That is the only thing they have taken away from us and rendered us useless and mentally ill. However, the real case is that this is where our power is. The feeling is scary because it is the ultimate connection to Source, which they are really scared of.

When I was in my deepest, darkest hole, let's call it the bottomless hole because it is exactly that, but it is something that can't be described either. Someone said something to me that sent me further down than I could bear. Well, obviously, I did bear it *somehow* because I am here, writing this to you.

They said to me that someone heals from trauma in a big community with love, support, being cared for, and touch/hugs. It broke me. Here I am, out in the country in isolation on 250 acres that almost killed me when two dogs mauled me by tug-of-war in the paddock with no one around, let alone the isolation itself. I was already struggling, and it sent me further down a spiral when they said this to me. The stark reality of my current reality at the time and what I am supposed to 'only be able to heal with love, support, being cared for, and touch/hugs.'

Let alone months prior, someone else told me that the three keys to longevity are Purpose, Social Connections (Love or Family), and Health. I also broke down. My health suffered greatly in the country. As a single mother, I couldn't function, having to drive 45 minutes to the beach, which was a life source for me of exercise, vitamin D, surfing, and walking barefoot on the Earth that cleansed my blood, keeping me happy and healthy. To go for a walk in the country, I need to cover up, wear gumboots, and ensure the ticks, snakes, bugs, and dust aren't at their peak. Yeah, that doesn't happen.

Hearing these things echoed in my mind for months, destroying me. I was a crying, blubbering mess 99% of the time. I was breaking down at the drop of a hat. I had crazy PTSD from the dog attack that would come in waves. I couldn't cope anymore.

The hardest thing was knowing that deep under it all, I was estranged from my family for doing what I loved. How on Earth does someone cope, let alone survive or live a normal life for 20 years without family, birthdays, or Christmas celebrations? Without a simple call in for a cup of tea to say hello? 20 fucking years. THAT is what was killing me. I couldn't believe it had been that long since I had lived without it. Let alone the stark realisation that I never had the warm, nurturing mother's love required for a healthy, resilient upbringing (not trauma-shock resilient!). It was the hardest thing I ever faced, knowing that those people who told me that to truly heal from trauma, you need touch, loving care, and kindness. They knew that I had none of that and hadn't for 20 years, and that somehow, in all of it, I was the only one that could bring me back to the surface of all this—alone. But how?! When 'they' said the only way to heal from trauma was with a tribe physically around you, and here I am out in the country in isolation on 250 acres?! WTF.

I had put myself into $320K worth of debt. I had thought things would continue the way they were going in my business; why wouldn't they? Forgetting that I had lost myself out in the country because I couldn't take care of myself in the way I needed to as a single mother on our own with no family or friends around, trying to get to hospital appointments, not being able to drive nor even walk after the dog attack, the floods and the level of mould it created, the animals, oh yeah, and caring for my daughter somehow in all that. I was so ashamed of how much debt I had accrued, and for months I sat in it, not knowing what to do and paralysed by how it made me feel. The shame clouded me on top of it all; I was drowning, trying to put on a brave face while dying inside, knowing people were sensing it too. I had run my business by showing up and teaching people how to live the life of their dreams, healing from their past, and turning their passion into their purpose. How the fuck was I supposed to do that in my state? Not to mention the PTSD from the dog attack that nearly killed me, peaking 8-9 months after the event, adding to the paralysis with everything compounded. I had put on weight, was unhappy living in the country away from civilisation, and the amount of driving was taking its toll. My now teenage daughter was ready to go out and socialize, what, with all the cows in the paddocks?

How on Earth was I supposed to get up and be this 'healer' when I was dying inside, ashamed of the position I had put myself in, and trying to pretend all was okay? Let alone knowing what was going on underneath—the estrangement from my family that was peaking at 20 years, and I couldn't believe it had been that long on my own, and... gah! The list goes on. I was a mess. How on Earth was I supposed to get up and be this 'successful healer' when every post I saw was about how you need family, friends, and health to be successful, or is it a facade? Yeah, trust AI to support you further into the spiral! Geeeezz!

I am all for honesty, integrity, and alignment. There was no way I was going to pretend everything was okay. But I was damn tired of talking about the trauma, the negative shit, the domestic violence, and all the relationship trauma I had endured. Can't I just talk about sunshine and roses and health and wellness? The things I love? Sure, but when was the last time I lived it? That's what I can't pretend to or would even try to do, so I found myself in a deeper hole than I had ever felt in my entire life. I didn't show up at my business. But when I did, I just talked about trusting your intuition, spirituality, and psychic readings; I barely spoke about anything else. I did the bare minimum for just over 12 months. It was all I *could* do. Ending my business was *not* an option. I hadn't come online for six years through blood, sweat, and tears—literally—to walk away now. *Not* an option.

Slowly, after that peak 9–10 month mark from the dog attack, I started to heal.

You Will Get Through Your Trauma; Go Easy on Yourself.

I slowly started to emerge from the worst of it, but the next few months were still tough. I ate baked beans on white toast because that was all we had in the cupboard. The debt was drowning me, and eating that sort of food only contributed to that. I couldn't turn up in my business and pretend everything was okay because it fucking wasn't! I am all for keeping it real, for goodness sake! But I wasn't going to talk about the negative shit either; I didn't want to. I did years of that, and I was tired of it. Bored of it even. But I simply didn't want to. So I didn't say anything. I felt so lost in my business. What the fuck was I supposed to talk about?

The shift began to take hold when I realised that the debt I had accumulated was me trying to heal on my own, in the middle of nowhere, isolated, with no family even caring to see if I was okay, and somehow raising a teenage daughter who was ready to go out, socialise, and mingle! I didn't even have petrol to drive us to town, let alone somewhere a teenager actually wants to hang out!

I had signed up with three different mentors after the dog attack. They were all very feminine, luxury-brand women. I love luxury for sure, but I realised it some months later. Subconsciously, I was looking for a surrogate mother. *Underneath, I was trying to heal.* Underneath was this desire to be loved and nurtured by the feminine, because I never had that growing up. Correction: I had that from my Nanna Edna, and yet she lived on the other side of the country, so I didn't have much of it, but it was a sliver of what that felt like, so I hung on to it like glue, and goodness knows what I would've done if I didn't have that. She passed away in 2014, and I feel her spirit's presence so much, especially these last few years living out here and going through what I have on this property in the country.

I found it so interesting that when I was lying in the hospital for five days awaiting surgery from the dog attack, the people who came and saw me were all the surrogate mothers I had accrued in my life unconsciously for the last 20 years living away from family. I remember asking one of them years ago why all my 'friends' were women much older than me. We all used to hang out, and it was great; we had fun, and I loved it at the time, but I remember having moments of wondering why they were all a good 10–15 years older. Her response at the time was that that was the consciousness I was around/holding/had as a young person. But I now see... the surrogate mother role was huuuuggggeeeeee. I am grateful for all those surrogate mothers, that is for sure. When they came and saw me in the hospital, I hadn't spoken to some of them for years, and then they were by my side. It was strange being alone for so long. Needless to say, neither one of them reached out after the hospital. That was also weird.

From those realisations of the surrogate mother role, I realised what was going on under the surface. I got through it. With lots of deep grief and huge tears constantly flowing, I somehow got through it. I am talking about 9–12 months of deep howling grief daily. It was insane when I look back on it, but it was all I could do; I couldn't stop the tears. I was determined not to let 'those' people tell me the only way to heal was with a tribe of people who loved me and were physically there to care for me, touch me, and love me. I didn't have that FFS, and I wasn't leaving my daughter to any of 'them'. So, somehow, I pulled myself out of it on my own. This isn't about a badge of honour for 'doing it on my own'. Of course, I asked for help. This is more about the fact that many of us Ancient Blooded Healers actually don't have anyone to ask for help from. We don't have *anyone*.

Even though my daughter was here, she may as well not have been. I, number one, wasn't going to dump any of this on her, even though I am sure she heard me crying most days, but I do remember losing it at her at times, which also isn't good. I would see couples and people 'complain' on social media about their hardships in business or otherwise, but they have family around and a caring husband by their side, and I just sank down and was like, 'Yeah, but I have no one going through this. And for 20 fucking years, I haven't.' That is what I kept tripping over—no birthday celebrations, no family get-togethers, no partner, and raising a daughter on my own. No nothing. Like WTF? Who does that?! *For twenty fucking years.* It truly was insane. But somehow, I got through it with time by letting myself be a blubbering mess for many days on end—*months on end*. And you can too.

I know that being in the mastermind with my mentor and working privately with her is what made me face this level of healing as I moved to the next level in my business as an Ancient Blooded Healer and found the path that I have to bring my gifts to the world, such as writing this to you here, right now. I remember seeing Russell Brunson's post, 'Entrepreneurship is the greatest form of personal development'. It is so true!

Shifting from just earning money in your business to acquiring wealth, knowing what to do to distribute that wealth to grow investments, and what to do as your business expands beyond you are not things taught in school, and again, unless your best friend and family members have done it, they are not the ones to be listening to or taking advice from when they have no idea whatsoever.

Who You Hang Around Matters.

There is a difference between healing yourself and having a side business where you do a few card readings here and there, a few reiki sessions, crystal healings, intuitive healings, or past life healings with a client and actually stepping into running a company or three, leaving your legacy, changing the world, and truly living your Life Purpose—the reason you were born.

When all feels lost, it isn't. But it definitely feels that way most of the time when you are walking the path of the hardest, most alone feelings in the world.

The reality is that the ones who feel most alone were not protected as children. They didn't have anyone standing before them protecting them when someone was bullying or abusing them; rather, the carer who was supposed to protect them was standing behind the perpetrator, supporting them! #ouch.

When you can heal this part of you that was abandoned in your deepest part of the most crucial time of need, you will finally start to feel like you're not walking up that huge ass mountain that is covered in spiky thorns. You don't even have any shoes on to get through it, so you are just stuck halfway up the mountain. You will soon discover that you not only have shoes on but that a pathway of flowers and fluffy green grass opens beneath you, leading you to a path down and around the mountain. You'll realise you never had to go up that way at all, meaning you never had to drag your past with you any further than where you are today. You never have to. The buck stops here. You can heal. And now.

You don't have to continue talking about it because you have realised how draining and tiring that is and how you keep re-activating it when you keep talking about it. You feel lost for quite some time because you don't know what else to talk about, and the stark realisation of how much it has consumed your life until this moment is, to say the least, heavy. You put down those backpacks with rocks inside and decide that from this moment forth, you are choosing to heal. You are choosing your future, not your past.

You want that freedom from all the pain, but then comes the reality of facing it, which isn't easy, but you, being your Ancient Blooded Healer lineage, know that to get to the other side, you have to face it. And that's something you're adept at, but deep down, you know it isn't easy. And yet, it is in your nature to do whatever it takes until it takes, because that is just how it is. You're not someone who gives up, even though you have ten times over in a second; you find a way and don't stop, no matter how many people try to take you down in the meantime.

Always Remember the Basics.

I slowly pulled myself out—I say slowly because I began remembering what I teach. I began remembering how I began. More so, I began remembering when I was happy doing all of this in the beginning. Sure, I lived within walking distance of the beach and had very easy access to all the things that make life convenient. (Country life is not for the faint-hearted!) But I also remembered some crucial facts that I live by, teach, and... well, forgot about amongst the deep, deep hole I was in.

Life Purpose Rules:

Do What You Can With What You Have.

Whatever You Do, Do It Consistently.

It Doesn't Need To Be Perfect, But You Do Need To Show Up.

The Messages Will Come Through <u>When</u> You Are Doing It.

The Next Step Will Be Shown To You <u>When</u> You Are Doing The Current Step.

These philosophies were how I built my business from the start. Coming back to them allowed me to move to the next level. I got stuck thinking I should be further along than I was, all while realising that a solid $15k–20k/month consistently with highs of up to $55k/month for the past four years at the time was actually fucking amazing. I wasn't seeing where I was at and was constantly judging myself for not being 'there yet'—where the fuck is 'there' even? Reaching your first $1,000/month, first $10,000/month, first $100k/month, first $1M/month, and beyond are all exactly the same. These philosophies apply at every level.

I began to remember the teachings of Amanda Frances and Grant Cardone that I had heard along the way at various points in time: Debt is not bad. It propels you forward. Billionaires have debts. Debt isn't bad; we are just trained in society to think it is. I originally purposefully got into debt too. After having a very unconscious experience with money when I was in my late teens to early 20s, when I got out of $20k debt due to an inheritance wiping my slate clean, I stayed debt-free for years. I didn't want to ever experience that again. I thought I was doing the right thing, which was a good thing—not having any debt! Too bad the time came when I wanted to get a car as a single mum, and because I had no credit history, they weren't interested! Gosh, it was full-on! I couldn't believe it.

Once my business got moving, I purposefully got a loan to help propel the business and start a credit history! I had a very good credit rating, too, so much so that AMEX contacted me for a Platinum business credit card, as I had a perfect 700+ credit rating. I said yes, realising this was an opportunity to propel me even further and that this was an invite-only event. Of all the times, as a single mum in the early days, I wished I had a credit card to get through those days of waiting for the next paycheck. I learnt to live without money. I learnt to live on nothing. I realised that the convenience of living in a town where I could walk to the beach when I couldn't afford petrol or go on a long walk with my daughter in the pram when she was younger were life savers and kept me sane.

Looking back through those times, I see how I did it back then on my own when my daughter was so young, when I was drowning in the depths of a $320k debt in 2022 and 'searching' for a way to get me out of it. I remember all these times when I didn't have a credit card or any debt, and not only how I did it *but how I longed for what I had now*. It slowly shifted me from resentment to gratitude as I looked at what I had now. I realised that being out here in the country, 20 minutes to the small local town and 45 minutes driving distance to anywhere else of decent civilisation, I had to be at this level in my business and have a very reliable, almost new car that I have now to even be in a position to live in such a place!

It was a big experience learning how to manage debt, work with debt, utilise it, and have a good credit rating. I felt like I was drowning in debt because I had all these negative societal and family beliefs about debt; that was the *only* anchor holding me back and drowning me. It wasn't the debt itself *but how I felt about it,* compounded by the family beliefs that I was untangling! It was like a big fishing net holding me down, but when I began to remember all of these crucial points, alongside the fact that I was fine until the dog attack and while I was 'trying to heal', I kept pressing 'buy'. I broke down bawling that moment back in August 2022 when I realised all the latest debt *was simply me trying to heal on my own out here in the country*, without all my healing resources, like the beach and simply being able to go for a walk, having been stripped away. Let alone the fact that 20 years had gone by without family gatherings, barely seeing them and living alone, wandering, almost lost most of the time for 20 fucking years.

I became grateful (after a good 6-9 months of processing this; *this wasn't an overnight shift*). I became grateful that I learnt these hard lessons with $320k in debt, not $320M. I became grateful that I could live out here in the country and experience this, realising you do have to be rich to live this way! Living on such property was abundantly rich in its own way. I always would say, 'Everyone dreams of a country lifestyle and having a property until they experience how much work it is and how out of the way of convenient civilisation it is.' I guess that is also why, in my big vision, I have always had many properties around the world, including a country estate and a beachside home. It has helped me refine what I want, get clear on what it takes to have such properties in life and the stepping stones of how to make that happen, what level of staff requirements I need, and what position I need to be in for this to be created as I go. The expansion, not the contraction, is what creates this.

In those 6–9 months after the darkest days, I began cleaning up my life and my business structure, hiring and firing in my business, and getting clear on what it takes to run a company the way I needed. I listened to Mr. Beast's podcast interview by Lex Fridman about six weeks after I had made these huge changes in my business, and it confirmed what I had known for years, let alone experienced. I had shared such with mentors in the past, and they shot me down, and it took me a bit to find my feet again with it, knowing that I needed to train people *my way to my structure in my unique business.* My Life Purpose business did not and will not fit into any current or future strategy that someone teaches me. It just won't. I tried, and it stifled me. It was just finding the right people to do this with! It takes time to find the right people and the right staff. I wish someone had told me that because, for years, I thought I was doing something wrong because I hadn't found the right staff yet. Oh, the paths we walk when creating the new! I had no idea what I was doing as I was figuring it all out, but somehow, I did. *Through blood, sweat, and tears, I did.*

It took me another two months after the business structure had changed before I could focus on my health again. For years, while living on the property, I struggled with myself on this issue. I would try to detox or eat healthily, only to realise why I couldn't do it. I knew the level of detoxing required and how it felt to need to function and hold everything together. It took me a while to realise that all the driving and just holding my business together by a thread, let alone that hard debt year, was too much stress to be thinking about detox at the same time. Single parenting, animals, and clients were already overwhelming. So, I had to let go and do what I could with what I had. I ate grounded, solid meats and foods and trusted this approach. It was literally what gave me the strength to get through the darkest days and pull myself back to some stability when I had none.

I Trust What I Am Guided To Do In Each Moment.

From food to sleep to work—all of it, I had to. I had nothing else to lean on, so I leaned deeper into trust, blocked out any naysayers', coaches', or mentors' judgement, and did what I knew how to do best. Incredible internet marketing guru Frank Kern kept popping up in my feed, as he does at the perfect time, and said something that changed the trajectory of my future. I had heard him say this years ago or sometime previously, but this time, it saved me, picked me back up, gave me confidence, and propelled me to my next level. 'What do I love? What am I good at? What has worked in the past? And repeat'. Right. Simple. Powerful. And GO TIME!

I was tainted by past mentors telling me not to use the word psychic or intuition 'because it attracts a certain type of person'. I screwed my face up and was like, 'What?! *That is me. Let alone what I do!*' I had copped it from her and my family and just kind of sank away over time. I stopped doing psychic readings, and every time I came back to doing them, I felt judged and held back. I didn't continue because I thought I was doing something wrong. I thought I couldn't charge high prices *and* continue doing psychic readings (the very thing I *love* and am damn good at). And then I remembered...

How about I just do whatever the fuck I want to do and find out how free I can be?

Along with Frank Kern's powerful and so damn simple message, which kicked me back into gear.

What do I love?

What am I good at?

What has worked in the past?

BOOM! It is my motto that I live by now! It brings me joy when I think about these questions because those times I was doing what I loved and doing that which I am damn good at, *and* has worked in the past, were when I was in full flow, doing what I loved, not caring what anyone thought of me, and just doing what I was intuitively guided to do. I began Psychic Readings again, which is what I love, and it opened up and led me back to all I do. I even felt firm in holding my ground in offering 'low-end' Psychic Readings alongside high-end long-term mentorship. I have something available for everyone because that is where my heart has always laid care and thrived—*on humans*, no matter their social or economic status.

I came to peace with myself, knowing that those high-end clients who judge me and don't want a bar of me because I also offer 'low-end' sessions are simply not the clients for me because they simply don't understand my true heart service. I have been in high-end circles and mentorships to hold this level of space, financial mindset, and energetics for expanding a thriving entrepreneurial world-changing system on this planet. I can choose to work with people who also want to work with me at any level. There is a skill in knowing how to hold space, talk to, and heal different calibres of people, which is a skill not many hold. The extremes. The Light and The Dark.

When You Are Paving A New Path,
You Have To Trust Yourself.

    I frequently think about how my signature program is' Trust Your Intuition' and how, in those years of mentorship and the first few years of building my business online, I dropped out of trusting myself! Ironic, I know! But as they say, 'We teach most of what we need to learn'. I also know that learning how to create an online business, stepping into CEO and what that entails, wealth creation, and remembering what I came online to do— brought me back to the path. Sure, you could look back in hindsight and say I could've done this differently, etc., but at the same time, I would not have learnt what I did if I hadn't gone through what I did, and I can safely say I needed to learn what I did for where I am going. I *know* that deep in my heart. As I mentioned before, I am glad I learnt what I did with $320k debt, not $320M, and it isn't even the money side of it—it is all the depth of trauma I had to heal and release to even start pulling myself out of the hole!

    I remember when I was thick in it. When AI showed me all the things to keep pushing me down, or perhaps you could look at it as though there were more triggers to deal with ultimately, but it didn't feel supportive at the time, that is for sure! I remember a post in my feed of a man crying in his car, the last photo he took before he topped himself, leaving a note to his family and friends. It was (and I am sure there is more to it, of course) because of his debt.

    He had no job and couldn't provide for his kids. It broke me. I *knew* that feeling all too well, and I felt more powerless because they mentioned his debt in the post. It wasn't much compared to mine, but the feelings were the same. I felt a need to share the truth about money, the way to pull out of debt, that it isn't the end of the world (but it feels like it at the time!), that bankruptcy isn't the only option (when you look at Frank Kern's advice of doing what you love), and that there is *always* a way.

It is definitely the trauma surfacing underneath it when you are in your darkest days about money. My purpose is to help people consciously feel and understand that it isn't the surface issue that is the issue. There is such a stigma around money in our society, and it is created on purpose to keep us small and feeling all the negative things most of society does.

We also have the power to change those feelings and perceptions. That consciousness encompasses all areas of life; this is Life Purpose, including money. It is the Base Chakra. Throughout my teachings, you will hear me refer to money a lot because you can't heal yourself, help yourself, or change the world in today's society without money. We need to change our perceptions around it so we can indeed take our power back and not take our lives. This requires you to be around people who get it, have been there, pulled themselves out of it, and can help you heal from it. Not judge you more for the situation you have found yourself in that makes you not want to be here anymore. A lot of good can come to the world with heart-based entrepreneurs creating wealth, and we need more of them, aka YOU.

The biggest key, which I will repeat, is that when you make the decision to change your life, be prepared for 18 months to 3 years' worth of healing ahead of you. I'll repeat it so you don't, at the 6-month mark, feel like you're not making headway because it is all falling to shit again, and you're wondering why you feel the dark spiral again. *Three* years, honey. It's okay; you're not going backward or failing. You're making progress. It's just a point in your timeline; you will get past this next point too. I promise. But you must surround yourself with those who get it and walk away from those who don't. You've outgrown them. Trust yourself enough to know that you will be perfectly guided without them because you will.

You're a Wisdom Walker.

The biggest Lightworkers on the planet have had the darkest paths. Trying to receive mentorship, wisdom, healing, or advice from anyone who has not walked through a hard past and come through it will do nothing more than make you doubt yourself, think you're crazy, and believe you cannot be healed, which is *not true*. It is just that the practitioner, mentor, or healer you are working with does not have the required skill set to help you in this situation and heal from your darkest path. What irritates me, infuriates me even, is when said practitioners tell the client they can't be healed, are 'cursed for life', that 'you'll just have to live with it' or 'turn it around on you'. What they should be saying is, 'I am not qualified to help you with this; let me recommend someone who is'. It is so simple to admit that it is beyond your capabilities or intuitive understanding. Yet, I have had countless clients come to me and tell me stories of this, let alone clients that have been stuck in past-life trauma because of a healing session that left them in it!

It is probably one of the hardest lessons to learn when you are coming into your wisdom and realising you are an Ancient Blooded Healer, healing from your past and knowing what you have walked through, to then try and receive mentorship from someone who does not understand that level of 'darkness, unconsciousness, and subconscious' or understands how to truly heal trauma, small or large. You can't just think your way around trauma. It doesn't work like that. Don't let anyone tell you there is something wrong with you or cop out and tell you to look deeper into yourself simply because they can't admit it is beyond their level of comprehension and capabilities. There is nothing wrong with you. You are fucking gifted. Now own it!

Your Wisdom is Here to Heal the World.

You have gone through what you have gone through for a reason. Even though you will spiral around and around at times—somewhat endlessly, it feels like—it will not feel like there is any reason. One day that clarity will drop in, and you will say, 'Yes! That's it! That is what I am meant to do!' And you will fly along on the biggest buzz of your life, and everything will be on fire. Then, in some way, it will all come 'crashing down', and you will wonder WTF all that was for in the first place and want to give everything up and walk away. Don't. Please don't. You have just broken through to a new level. Know this, recalibrate, take your time finding your feet on this new level, and know you are just expanding, which requires everything to collapse as new structures are built to house the next level expansion. Always remember this.

You Are A Wisdom Walker.

Your very existence is here to change the world, heal others, heal yourself, and live the life you've always dreamt of. Find the courage to want to heal, to heal, to surround yourself with those on a similar path, to walk in solitude for as long as it takes, for as long as you need to, and to create the life you dream of.

Chapter 5

Your Values Activate Your Life Purpose

And keep you sane!

Your values are how you discover your boundaries, and your boundaries are what separate you from the rest of the world—not walls, but boundaries. When we are not conscious of our Values, this is where enmeshed, unhealthy, and toxic relationships come in and will continue to come in, whether in our careers, personal lives, or anywhere else.

Your Values are what make you, well, you.

Your Values keep you in clarity and alignment.

It is what you believe in.

It is what you stand for.

It is what makes you happy.

It is what brings you alive.

And it will be the first thing you drop. The flame of your life goes out, and the twinkle in your eyes turns black when someone says something nasty to you.

I hear many people saying that 'you have low self-worth' if you are affected by what others say. I beg to differ. I believe that we are all highly Clairsentient beings, and we feel things differently and deeply. It is a normal human trait and psychological factor to care what others think of you!

It is our first port of call for survival as children—to be accepted and loved; otherwise, we are kicked out of the safety of the tribe and eaten by a wild lion! It is normal to look for validation and acceptance in others. There is nothing wrong with you if you care what others think of you! It is why you get up in the morning, look good, and do what you do. We thrive on positive regard, which is why we are cut deeply when spoken to negatively to our face, behind our backs, online, or abandoned in our time of need.

The saying 'words can never hurt you' is not true. Words are energy, and energy is what makes up this reality. It is why it is so important to understand how to clear negative energy from your body, mind, Soul, and physical environment. Because words spoken to your face or behind your back cut your energy field open, and this is the basis of a psychic attack. It doesn't even need to be intentional because, as an Ancient Blooded Healer, you feel people talking about you, positively or negatively. You feel the slightest change in the energetic atmosphere, just like animals do.

Your values are what keep you on track with your Life Purpose. They are what keep you in alignment. They are what stop you from making 'bad' decisions. They are what stop you from staying in unhealthy relationships and situations. Your Values give you your moral compass.

Values are so important, and yet we are not taught this as children in school, and unless we have very conscious parents, we are usually not taught by our parents either.

Values are things that are important to you. They are what you love to do. They are direct communications from your Soul. They are showing you who you are.

Your Values are endless and limitless and can always be expanded upon and given revision, strength, and conscious awareness to improve your life. If anything is wrong in your life, the first place to check is whether you have moved away from your Values.

As an example, your values may be:
- Healthy eating and detoxing regularly
- Exercising

- The type of music that you enjoy that makes you feel a certain way that makes you—you
- Believing in God or Spirituality and taking those disciplined practises as part of your daily life
- What you believe in
- Living your life to a certain standard
- Living your life in a certain way with certain routines
- Not tolerating being spoken to in a certain way
- Wearing clothes, diamonds, or household items that are ethically sourced
- Drinking only a certain water
- What is important to you
- Who you hang out with and surround yourself with
- Family
- Love

The hardest thing for an Ancient Blooded Healer is valuing family when you are the scapegoat for your family. It can cause us to stay in unhealthy, toxic patterns and relationships (including the family system!) way longer than is healthy for us. It is the cause of deep loneliness, anxiety, and panic. Over time, with great healing and power journeys for the Ancient Blooded Healer, we do find our way, find our own families, and live our own lives. It is possible, but it is not usually an easy road to get there. Hang in there, precious one. #iseeyou

We may come across people on our path as Ancient Blooded Healers who put us down for living a certain way, and in a need to fit in, we dull who we are to do just this. Obviously, we lose our spark and lives in the long term. I bet if you are reading this somewhere along the line, you have done this or are doing this right now. One of the hardest things to do is to value yourself enough to know that your own validation and love are enough. Yet it is one of the hardest things to do, especially when you are on your own. Don't let anyone tell you otherwise. They have no idea what you have been through, let alone how much you have had to go through on your own and still are.

Most of the time, the people telling you that you need to get over it are either:

- Unconscious
- Have never had to walk in your shoes.
- Do not understand trauma. Remembering 'trauma' doesn't have to be a big catalytic event! It can be a 'tiny' thing that scars us for life.
- Have never gone through a traumatic space like you have.
- Are surrounded by family, friends, and loved ones 99% of the time.

Now, while there is nothing wrong with that, when we are healing, it is important to realise who you are receiving advice from, talking to, or even telling your issues to. I have even experienced a point with my therapist where I realised, after a few sessions towards the end, that she doesn't get the depth of what I speak of. She lives a completely different life from mine, and it was a dawning moment in my healing journey when I became quiet and wrote my books instead.

As an Ancient Blooded Healer, there comes a point where you realise that people do not understand what you do, who you are, or what you are saying at times. People will call me narcissistic, egotistical, and full of myself when I say that we are more conscious and energetically understanding than most of the population on the planet. It is our gift; it is who we are. It is not any of those labels; it is a pure fact. It is a hard, lonely pill to swallow when we realise this, and while it can be a curse, this is the transmutation from your curse to your gift. This is your Mastery.

The next phase of your Mastery is understanding how to 'be in society' without being looked at like you're weird when you talk. It is knowing who to say what to. It is knowing when to channel your gifts in the right direction so you don't blurt stuff out randomly (cue weird looks and the doorway for daggers behind your back to come in). It is knowing when you have truly outgrown some friendships and relationships and when it is time to move on.

Your Values Keep You Connected To Yourself.

It is very easy to drop your values when you are trying to fit in, be liked, or be accepted by someone or society. However, it isn't long before the spark of your Soul either disappears forever and you don't want to be on this Earth anymore, or you become lifeless robotic zombies following the orders of another after the resentment fades. Or we snap out of it, shake up the entire status quo of our system, and break free, slowly coming back to life.

When this happens, we become super clear on what our values are. We learn what we love and what we drop to try and fit in, and the ironic thing is that even though we drop what we love, drop our values, and try to fit in, they still don't like, value, or approve of us anyway! It wasn't about us!

Slowly, we start to remember what we love, care about, and *value*. We begin to pull ourselves back up out of the Soul grave we dug ourselves, and the most amazing thing is that we *eventually* come out stronger and clearer than we ever have before. Our connection to ourselves, our Soul, and what we love is a bond that is stronger than before. We are conscious of what we love; we are conscious that this is us, and we love ourselves more deeply, consciously, and that—isn't that what we are looking for? To be consciously loved, adored, and appreciated for who we truly are?

You step into a bond with yourself that you eventually look back on and are grateful for what you have been through because you wouldn't be who you are today without it. And yet, when you are in it, you do not know how you are going to get through this moment, what the point is, or how on Earth you ended up *here!* If you are in that situation, know that everything is going to be okay, you will be alright, you are exactly where you need to be (even though it makes *no* sense whatsoever), you didn't deserve what happened to you, and you will get through this, one breath at a time. I promise you.

Your Values Will Lead You To Your Life Purpose.

When you start to anchor in what you love, you will open the pathway to your Life Purpose. Sometimes we know what we love to do daily, weekly, monthly, or annually, and yet it can be the last thing left in the pile after all the chores of life are done. If you want to switch your life around, find your joy, and live your Life Purpose, start making the things you love a priority, and you will be surprised at how fast the Universe responds in kind. Opportunities will line up that would never have happened otherwise; your energy will suddenly come back; you will feel alive and refreshed; and you will wonder how you ever stopped doing those things you love.

Some people tell me they don't know what they love doing or that they tried it and it didn't work for them. Most of the time, these people don't step outside their comfort zone, give up way too soon, don't take risks to put their true heart's desire into action, don't see that what they are doing right in front of them is actually what they love, and are too scared to leave the family system. These are the ones that will also tell you not to do what you love and usually have a closed mindset. These are not the people to tell your dreams to. It would be questionable to continue hanging around or working with them. I will quickly move away from people who tell me they settled for less than their dreams, and it all makes sense to me why they are clearly in unsatisfactory relationships. But, hey, that is how society is trained.

There are a few Ancient Blooded Healers who value their happiness, values, and dreams so much that they would rather stay single until the right person comes along. They have such a deep faith that their divine counterpart is somewhere on this planet, even though, at times, they look to 'what they could've had' with marriage, children, or the 'white picket fence dream' throughout their past. (Wait, does that even exist? Oh, that's right, more programming.) They are divinely satisfied with their Purpose work, doing what they love, and following their hearts. That, my love, is threatening for most people in society.

It's okay to stand out in the crowd.

It is okay to do what you love.

It's okay to follow your heart.

It is okay to believe that there is MORE for you.

It is okay to only do what you want to do.

It's okay to hold a strong and huge vision about how the world 'should be' or 'could be' and what your Purpose work requires of you to bring this to fruition.

It's okay to go against what everyone says you 'should' do.

It is okay to hold firm in believing what is possible for your life; in fact, it is required.

If you are to live what you truly believe is possible—what you see in your heart and Soul of the life you are meant to live, dear Ancient Blooded Healer—it is required that you hold this for as long as it takes, taking *daily dedicated aligned action* at the same time.

It is essential that you only surround yourself with those who also believe in you and lift you up. Anything other than this is death to your Soul unless you want to live as a zombie with a soulless human body walking around as an empty shell. No, I didn't think so.

Your Values Are The Gateway To Your Heart.

Your values are what keep your heart open.

Your values are what keep you happy.

They are what help you heal when your heart is broken.

They are what keep you alive on this planet; they are what keep your Soul engaged in your life, and not only do they make you—YOU, but they are also the seed of your joy. They keep you youthful and will be the fastest thing to pull you back on track, illuminate your next steps, and strengthen who you are.

The only thing that makes you *not* want to do this again is the grief you need to feel to heal from whatever event unfolded or surfaced from years ago. Take the time to let yourself deal with this and come back to the truth of who you are.

If complete Soul satisfaction and pure satiation of your Life Purpose and Destiny are strong values for you, you won't do anything other than follow your Heart, and that gateway is held open by your Values.

If you are lost in your Values and don't know what you love doing, use this *Healing Protocol For Your Soul*:

For 30 days, take your favourite journal or pen and paper and ask these questions (listed below) over and over again. For example, ask the question, then write whatever comes to mind.

Then ask the question again and write whatever comes to mind.

You are repeatedly asking the same question over and over again. It might seem like nothing comes out, or it is just simple 'plain' stuff. You may even write 'I don't know' for some of it.

When you continue to ask it repeatedly in a session, writing the next thing that comes out, eventually, it will drop into some GOLD that you didn't even know existed inside of you or let yourself ever dream of before now.

Healing Protocol for your Soul Questions are:

- If I had no responsibilities, what would I be doing with my time?
- Am I exhausted? What do I need to do to replenish this? (If you are exhausted, it can take a little unravelling to return to what you

love with joy and gusto. Replenish and train yourself to be comfortable in the 'nothingness space of not knowing' for however long it takes.)
- What do I love?
- Who do I love?
- What does my Heart want?
- If I could travel anywhere, where would I go, and what would I do?

You can choose to ask one question a day or ask them all every day. If you are busy and strapped for time, do one daily. If you have the space to do all of them, I recommend taking the time to do this. Ask the questions Monday through Friday, taking the weekends off. Count the 30 days, including the weekends. Taking the weekends off from the protocol makes it manageable and allows integration of the energy change.

This is such a powerful process—and repeating it daily for 30 days? Get ready for major changes, a deep acceleration of your Life Purpose, and a renewed sense of energy and self that the world hasn't seen yet. Prepare to become someone unrecognisable—but someone your heart is so fulfilled by— that suddenly everything you've ever dreamt of and worked so hard for in your entire life suddenly shows up, just like magic. You have known all along that this is how it was meant to have been. And all it took was some deep, honest, Soul-touching conversations with your Soul!

You see, coming back to doing what you love and finding what you love can be the simplest thing. If you've been busy for quite some time, you might have forgotten how much you love making meals from scratch for satisfaction, taste, and soul nourishment. If you have moved out of your old routines for whatever reason, you may have forgotten how a 'simple' walk on the beach nourishes your Soul. Slowly, slowly, you start coming back to yourself.

It isn't that you will be ecstatic about those things when you 'come back to them'—I mean, you could be, of course! However, what it does is repair and reconnect the connection back to yourself, back to your Soul. The more you do it, the stronger that connection becomes. As this connection strengthens, you will find that ideas, opportunities, synchronistic flow, and intuition all become stronger and usually more solid. You remember who you are and what you love. You will feel ever more protective about your sacred space and these sacred practises, rituals, and routines that nourish your Soul and make you—you.

Who Were You Before You Fell?

That light-hearted, joyful you, the one who loved life and all that it entailed. As we move through different developmental points in our lives, I am not just talking about when we are kids! We move through different age stages at every age in our lives. These particular age developmental stages, compounded with what happens at different times of our lives (e.g., death, marriage, babies, career changes, moving countries—all kinds of things), create layers of change, or 'metaphysical scar tissue', as I call it.

When you are coming out of a rough situation, out of a time in your life where you have lost yourself and are just realising this, trying to get back on track, or trying to pull yourself out of a deep black hole, please be gentle with yourself in understanding how many layers there are here. Please know you *will* get through this, but it comes in time, with dedicated turning up to the next thing you know you need to do and allowing yourself to do it without judgement so you can start gaining traction rather than staying stuck where you are. Even 'stuck' isn't a thing. It is a bit like 'feeling numb'—that too is a feeling and means you are 'in it' and it is moving. We often think that 'feeling happy' is all there is (in a way) and forget that 'numb' or 'stuck' is also a feeling. When we are feeling it, it is because we are feeling it! It is moving through us, just like happiness or sadness. Do not underestimate the power of consciously recognising that all these *are* feelings. It is okay to be 'adrift' for as long as it takes to find the current that picks you up and takes you in a new direction after being 'lost' for so long. In the meantime, be okay with being 'adrift'. Let God carry you. Let the Universal flow move forth through you. You have always been a part of it, and that has never left you. Let go and let this be true. It might seem like so long you will be adrift and that it will never end, but if you can allow it, one day, I promise, you'll start to see signs that the current has picked you up and is taking you closer to shore. One breath at a time, one thing at a time.

After these 'metaphysical scar layers' become conscious and accepted, deep healing will ensue, bringing you into acceptance of a different stage of your life. This can come with deep grief and a realisation that what and who you once were and the things you once loved are not the same anymore and that your life has truly changed. You may not know what 'makes you happy now', who you really are any more, or what to do now, but you will find what does in this next stage and phase of your life, I promise you.

Give yourself the grace and time to allow this letting go of your old life to come into your new one. We often find that the things we have been grieving for in the 'now' are actually lost hopes and dreams that never were or were going to be, not what was. When you realise this and come into this clarity, you will see that you are just on a stepping stone phase and that those things that truly matter to your Heart and Soul *can and will happen*. It's just that it hasn't happened *yet*.

Chapter 6

Understanding Your Ancient Blooded Healer Gifts

The biggest part about Ancient Blooded Healers having spiritual awakenings is the number of visions and 'bad' and 'scary' experiences they tend to have with their intuition. I have had many clients come to me over the years and share stories of how they would see murders and car accidents in places before they happened. It would freak them out, scare them away from their intuition, and make them even more scared to pursue their talents and abilities with their intuitive skills. They were afraid and didn't understand why they were seeing such horrifying scenes!

What I found time and time again with clients is that the reason they see such horrific visions or premonitions is because *their intuition is trying to get their attention!* Once these clients began their journey to increase, hone, and learn their intuitive skills and then step into teaching this healing work in some capacity, these visions stopped happening! They still had intuitive visions, but they weren't of horrific scenes that would freak them out! Their intuition was just grabbing their attention, especially if they had been ignoring the subtle signs to learn and increase their skills about it. Once they began their diligent work on pursuing intuitive training, their intuition didn't have to grab their attention so much because they were on the path and following it.

Pursuing your intuitive training keeps you sane because you understand and learn about the energy, rather than falling in a great heap, wondering whether you're Arthur or Martha, piled on top of all the energy you are carrying, but you're not sure what is yours and what isn't! You're not going crazy; you're just highly intuitive, sense everything, and have very important and incredible skills that need training. That's all!

Everyone is psychic. Everyone is intuitive. For some, it just comes more naturally, just like people who love swimming will be naturally better swimmers than someone who is scared of water! However, anyone can train in any skill; the more they love it, the better they are. Think about it: things you have no interest in or care for, you truly don't want to learn about, and even if you did, you wouldn't be that great at them because you don't really like them. For naturally born Ancient Blooded Healers, we love this stuff, so of course, we are going to be better at it and have a stronger, clearer connection than most.

You have a zillion tarot and oracle card decks, give readings all the time, or perhaps even already do this professionally, mentor, coach, and have clients in some way, shape, or form already, and if not, it's on your mind to! If cards are not your thing, I bet you're the most inspiring and positive person in your 'group' and that people always comment on how much you help them. I bet you have also heard, 'I don't know why I just told you that; I have never told anyone that before!' After they just finish telling you their life story! A natural-born Healer—that is what you are and why that happens! By the way, the 'dumping' of people just telling you their life story, usually without invitation, starts to decrease when you begin pursuing this line of work in some way, shape, or form. It is another way your intuition guides you through honing your skills in this area as a Clairvoyant, Healer, or some kind of Spiritual Teacher, Coach, or Mentor. You're born to do this work, or you just wouldn't be here reading this.

So why hone your skills as a Healer? Intuitive? Psychic? Mentor? Coach? Spiritual Teacher? Well, number one, it comes easily to you—you love this stuff! You thrive on learning about this! You do it regardless of whether you are making a career of it or not. You will find that when the visions increase, the number of people who 'tell you their life story out of the blue' or when people randomly say to you, 'You should be doing this for a career', You're an Ancient Blooded Healer, and this is calling you to pursue it. Plain and simple!

Why else is it wise to hone your intuitive skills? Because you feel it all anyway, absorbing it like a sponge. Honing your skills and healing your traumas, thus clearing your energy field on deep levels, is how you not only become more psychic but are also able to tell what your energy is from someone else's energy. What are the Earth's energies? What is surfacing for you, them, the Earth, or something else? You become more conscious instead of a crazy mess of energy that sometimes leaves a sour taste in your mouth and makes you wish you weren't so awake sometimes! You are clearer, more confident, and have more energy and direction. You know who you are and where you're going. Well, most of the time! It is normal to have waves of feeling like you have no idea whatsoever as to why you are doing any of this and want to walk away from it all. Remember, this is a breakthrough point. It is normal to feel this at times alongside a deeper undertone of Purpose and know that you need to continue this path because this is what you were born for. Whatever *that* is! But you know, at the same time. And that is all the thread of inkling you need to follow.

Honing your skills is the fastest way to stop unpleasant visions and set healthy boundaries with people who continue to drain your energy long after you have stepped into this work professionally. Even if you choose not to do this professionally in some way, shape, or form, honing your skills leads you to your Life Purpose. Healing deep past lives and childhood traumas clears your energy field. There is only so much chakra clearing, meditation or Reiki treatment you can do before you're ready for the deeper work of past life, childhood, inter-dimensional, and original wound clearings. You become highly clear in your intuitive faculties when you clear out deep traumas. It is like releasing the heavy, brick-loaded backpacks and cloaks you've been carrying around and wearing. When you 'put these down' by healing your old past wounds and traumas, you attract a different reality because your vibration has changed energetically. Those heavy 'dark and unconscious' wounds are not energetically sitting in your energy field, body, and psyche, attracting the same dense unconscious reality. Your intuitive senses are heightened and clear because the cloaks and bricks are not in the way anymore. This enables you to read your subconscious and other people's subconscious more clearly. You are highly psychic anyway; honing your skills makes you *clear* about what energetic threads are going on. You become acute in knowing if they are yours or someone else's, which makes you an incredible Healer because you become so clear in what is going on in someone's life to help them. It is your gift. Honing it makes you very unique and powerful in what you do. You're not crazy, but you may feel that way if you don't hone and understand your gift with in-depth training.

Different Kinds of Visions:

Your Clairvoyance is a part of your intuition of Seeing, ClairSeeing, or ClearSeeing. You see clearly when your Third Eye is open. You can see straight to the truth; you usually have a photographic memory. You look up or to the top right or left when thinking of something you are trying to say, explaining something, or downloading a message through your intuition. You speak in colours and pictures and see the big picture of any situation. You see beauty all around you, and you love seeing pretty sunsets and sunrises. You also love nature and what it shows you. You *need* nature to soothe your Soul, and being surrounded by beauty makes you feel loved, whole, and complete.

Your Clairvoyance is where you 'see visions', and there are different types of visions, just as there are many different ways to 'see'. Many people think they are not Clairvoyant because they cannot 'see ghosts' or colours. And yet, I bet they see 11:11 almost every day! Your Clairvoyance is not just what you see with your Third Eye. It is what you see with your physical eyes as well, hence the number sequences, feathers falling in front of you, or gold coins found in places you wouldn't usually find gold coins. Your Clairvoyance can be internal as a vision, which can feel like or look like a memory when you think about it. Your Clairvoyance is composed of your three eyes—two physical eyes and one internal eye.

Your Clairvoyance is based on the signs you see in your everyday life (physical eyes). Whether that be the repeating numbers on clocks, car number plates, receipts, or other places, you are being shown messages. You are seeing with your three eyes: your two physical eyes and your one spiritual eye. You may also see repeating literal signs everywhere, on power poles or the backs of cars, telling you to go to a yoga class or surf lessons, for example.

When a vision happens, it is like you are witnessing a scene from a third-person point of view. You can also be the person in the scene, witnessing it, or the person you are today, experiencing it. You could be seeing it in your mind, like when you think about a picture or a memory. You could be witnessing the vision 'externally' in a location in front of you or in a different location in the world. When witnessing a vision, it almost comes with a feeling; it can be described as a daydream or 'zoning out'. Pay close attention when you 'snap out of it' and train yourself to remember what you were just witnessing or being shown.

Dreams

Dreams are also deeply connected to your Clairvoyance.

Sleeping Dreams. When you wake up from a dream, you may or may not remember it. The best way to build your skills at interpreting your dreams is to write them down as soon as you wake up, even when they don't make sense. The very act of putting pen to paper and writing what you can remember, even when you write, 'I don't remember my dream, but I know I was dreaming!' Allows your intuition to become 'real' in our 3D world. Your intuitive muscles get stronger, and over time, you learn to interpret your intuition—not just your dreams but your entire intuitive vocabulary. Commit to writing your dreams down for 18 months and watch your world change!

It is common for Ancient Blooded Healers who start working with me in private mentoring or who step into Reality Awareness to have sleeping dreams of meeting a caste of Priestesses, Wizards, and Healers, all dressed in white or gold, and being ordained into these teachings. I love it when I hear these stories of their sleeping journeys, as it always confirms and leaves me in awe, no matter how often I hear it, of the realms beyond this reality that are as real as the book or device you're holding in your hands to read this.

Nightmares are simply the subconscious trying to get your attention. Where are you not paying attention to your intuition in the daytime? What is going on in the household you are in? Are there unhealthy, toxic relationships, constant arguments, or uncomfortable conversations that need to be had? Do you or any household members take drugs or drink a lot of alcohol? All of these will have an effect on you or anyone else in the house, including children. Clean up the energetic and physical environment, have those hard, honest conversations, and follow your intuition where you are being guided. Just like clients who come to me and have confronting, usually horrific, scary visions, it is their intuition trying to get their attention and follow their spiritual calling. Nightmares are the same; they wake you up to something. What is that?

Seeing people out of the corners of your eyes in your home or out and about at other places usually happens in 'waves' of time. It will be for a few days straight, and then you won't seem to notice this anymore. While there are many reasons and layers for 'seeing people out of the corners of your eyes' or seeing shadows and ghosts in general, the 'waves' of seeing shadows and ghosts like this, which I have noticed with myself and my clients over the years, occur when there is a portal opening on Earth or in the Cosmos somewhere, or when 'the veils are thin', as we call it. It can be times of the year that are 'predicted dates', like on Solstice, Equinox, Eclipse or it can be when big solar flares enter our atmosphere. It can happen anytime, of course, and it is always important to check your energy field, clear and cleanse your home, and close any portals if they are open. I teach this deeply in my Heal The Land Course, which is also a bonus in my Trust Your Intuition to Become a Certified Intuitive Healer and Life Purpose Activator Course. Over the years, of course, I have noticed them, cleared and cleansed the energy, but also just knew it was bigger than us, that parallel realities and dimensions collide, that portals open and close, and that staying focused, present, and grounded where you are, alongside claiming and cleansing your space, is your greatest protection.

Life Purpose Dreams. These are your goals, the vision and dream of your life that you know you're meant for. It is important to know that this vision, that deep knowing of what and how your life is supposed to be, is there for a reason and is a signpost for you to live for. Keep going *until.* It is meant for you; otherwise, you wouldn't have this vision!

Having dreams, visions or pulling oracle or tarot cards of someone dying doesn't necessarily mean that you are seeing their death. This can also be your intuition showing you that they are going through a huge transition in their life—that might feel like death to them (a relationship breakup, for example), but it is also that a part of them is also dying. Essentially, they are going through a huge life change and leaving an old life behind, so it would be like a death to them in a way. This is the same for seeing Crows, Ravens, Bats, or dead animals in a short space of time. An old section and part of your life are dying, and a new one is being reborn. Wolves represent the death of old consciousness that you are shedding from your life and no longer need. 'Seeing death' doesn't always mean literal death, although it can for sure, but once you start to understand the language of your own intuition through healing your past traumas and honing your intuitive skills, you'll start to learn the difference between what your intuition is actually communicating to you and what you are being shown.

When you are healing and a memory comes back to you from your childhood, it shows you where this particular trauma or incident began. It can have a layered effect, meaning that it can have what I call 'scar tissue' layers right up until your current age today. The original wound creates an imprint in your body or psyche and creates your reality from this perspective. You may have encountered similar situations along the road of your life, all of which 'pile upon' this original wound like scar tissue. You do not need to clear out each layer to get to the wound, but sometimes it can unravel like that. 99% of the time with my clients, we go straight to the core wounding (usually in less than 10 minutes!) and unravel from there. Once the core wounding is healed, the other layers disintegrate 'on their own' or with tears and memories surfacing for 2–9 weeks after our initial session. When clients come to me or people find Reality Awareness, an 18-month healing cycle ensues from when they originally found me. Everything will unravel and become conscious. Everything will surface. The darkest and hardest emotions—the biggest howling grief cries you've ever experienced—will happen. If you let yourself go there, that is. It is how we truly heal. Let yourself. You are safe as you grieve. There is nothing wrong with you. You are healing. Being privately mentored by me takes this to another level, and another 18-month cycle takes a deep shift in consciousness, and your Life Purpose accelerates when working 1:1.

It is important to understand that along the timeline of your life, there are certain key points that are 'easier' to heal through certain windows of time. However, I don't know if 'easy' is the right word! Most of the time, it feels like a mental breakdown! Life will feel like it is falling apart—that nothing you do works anymore, that something needs to change, that you're bored with life, that you've just gone through a huge relationship breakup, a death in the family, or that something completely collapses and you didn't see this one coming! At these times, there can be multiple timelines affecting this point in your life right now. You're not falling apart; the old systems, modalities, and ways of doing your life are changing. That is all. There will be the core wounding of your childhood or past life, plus the layers of 'repeating' experience since that moment in time when it first happened. This, combined with your age on the timeline, plus past lives converging at a point. That is why it literally feels like you are losing your mind. It is common to feel this way when trauma is surfacing and releasing from your body. It is important to be around experienced healers at this time when you are going through such a huge timeline convergence and purging experience in your life. You're not losing it; you're losing your old life, that is all. The old skin is shedding. Grieve, cry, and take care of yourself as much as you can, for as long as you need to, during this time. You will get through this, even though, at the time, it will not feel like it.

I realised in my darkest time of isolation from the outside world when I found myself living on a 250-acre property in the Noosa Hinterland, Queensland, Australia, that I actually liked people! Living in suburbia, with the area becoming more and more built up, I came to a place where I was over it all and wanted out. Well, that was granted to me, and I found myself 'in the middle of nowhere', and on 250 acres no less—lots of space, no people, and plenty of cows! It was great at the start, but then the driving became tiring, and running a business, single-mumming with a teenage daughter, and all the animals took their toll on me. It sent me into the deepest spin of healing family rejection and trauma I had never felt before. I had to be isolated to face it! That entailed times when I lost it in my car while putting it away in the garage (the sheds are away from the house on the property). It was windy as anything, and I had the car still turned on. I began screaming as loud as I could. I was at my breaking point. Everything had built up. I broke down. Hard. I was screaming and screaming and screaming, and it was like the same scream from when the dogs attacked me, but it was 'invasion' screaming. I was screaming so hard that it was releasing the trauma out of my body, and I could see a huge tube being released from me that had been invading my energy for goodness knows how long. Sound heals. And I was grateful for the very windy day and my V8 for covering the sounds of my screams that day. Maybe being out 'in the middle of nowhere' is good for some things.

It was so hard. It was my 20th year living away from family across state lines since I left when I was 18. That 20-year timeline point is, of course, another crucial timeline element. This was the greatest timeline convergence I have ever felt, and I wouldn't wish it upon anyone; it was horrendous! And yet, the greatest gift came out of it, of course. Alone. Aloneness. Being Alone. The thing I was most ashamed of in my life—aloneness—became my greatest ally and gift—the gift of being alone.

I had been alone for a long time. Except for having my daughter around, I had always lived alone; rarely had I lived with anyone since I was 21, and then once I had my daughter at 25, I only lived with her. Being on the property made me realise just how alone I was. I loved it at times, but when the exact 20-year mark was approaching when my family told me I had to go to TAFE or University and study something because working in a pet shop (I was managing it, not just working in it!) wasn't good enough, it sent me into the second darkest night of my Soul I have ever experienced. I couldn't believe that for 20 years, I had been living away from family, interstate, never experiencing family gatherings, birthday celebrations, weddings, funerals, births, christenings, Christmases, New Years, etc. How does someone miss out on all those things? I had just been doing it. How did 20 years go by? How had I been single-parenting for 13 years at that point? I couldn't just 'fly home and see them'. I never seemed to have enough money to make ends meet as a single mum, and then learning and running my own business and a company—holidays? What is that?

I was breaking down. The biggest breakdown of my life. It was nine months after the dog attack, converging with the 20 years of living away from home, stuck out on the property, and I had just woken up that I had added another $200k to my debt in less than four months, trying to heal on my own with PTSD from the dog attack with all of this converging…and let's not forget the floods on the East Coast of Australia at this time that laid for constant rain and mould—I lost it, to say the least. The healers I used to see wouldn't answer my messages; no one was replying, and I was turning 38. I didn't even look at my Facebook timeline to view the hundreds of birthday messages. I just couldn't face it, which is unusual for me. I didn't hear from my family; they just 'see me online' and don't even think to ask if I am okay, and meanwhile, behind the scenes, I can't stop crying and breaking down. Insane. Phew. It was… Huge.

On my birthday, by 6 p.m., it dawned on me. All day, I had been waiting, expecting them to turn up for my birthday. That was a 5- to 6-hour flight and then a 3-hour drive away, mind you. And all day I had been waiting for them to turn up, but I didn't realise it. It was so real. By 6 p.m., I was like, 'WTF?' I snapped out of it. I was subconsciously waiting for them to all turn up and surprise me for my birthday. It was so real, so strong, and when I became conscious of this 'waiting', I broke down. I have not cried so deeply and so hard before. It was old, it was (from when I was) young, and it was so core-deep that I knew the moment I became conscious of the 'unconscious waiting all day' that my inner toddler was waiting for someone to come and get her out of the cot, howling her eyes out, screaming out not to be left alone, and No. One. Came. #ouch

20 fucking years. Alone. And on my 38th birthday, that marked 20 years since they told me what I was doing wasn't good enough and that I needed to do better, and I left instead, driving across Australia when I was 18 and never going back. That timeline convergence of my inner toddler was huge. Crying it out as a toddler (or any age child) leaves detrimental effects on the child and scars them for life, as we can greatly see. Obviously, it was my time to heal this deep, core wound. Facing the pain of that level of abandonment and aloneness was insane. The reality is that most of the older generation didn't know better and were taught, as a society, 'That is how to raise kids'. No, definitely not, and it is the most damaging thing that can be done to a child. I am sure there are others, but let's stay on topic.

I became so ashamed around this time because so many had family and friends, constant photos of family and friends, celebrations, and people sharing that 'to be successful, show me your friends and family'. Well fuck, thanks, AI, for sending me down the spiral some more! I felt so ashamed, and how could I possibly be successful in the world if I had cut contact with family members, let alone chosen to walk away from them and most friendships because of the same abuse and turmoil? It took me quite some time to overcome this. The next nine months saw me deeply fall in love with who I am. Jeff Brown and Dr. Jaiya John's words echo deep love from my Soul and acceptance that it is okay to walk away from relationships, including family, if they do not support your highest vision and only serve to put you down or demean you. I knew deep down inside of myself that what I was doing was right—that to stay around relationships, no matter who they were, that only laughed loudly to my face or behind my back at what I was doing or put me down for what I did—to walk away from them was right. And yet, I held such judgement and shame because I didn't have family and friends because of this! I was alone, raising my daughter with our healthy ways of living, breathing, and philosophies about life. For many years prior, and when my daughter was young, I was proud to be living this way. But as time passed and more people said more things to me as I built my very public business online, their words, judgements, and the 'if you continue, we can't be together' chipped away at my Soul. Of course, I chose my Soul, but it scarred me, and I found myself alone and hurt.

For many years before becoming a mother and after quitting drugs, I thrived on being alone. I would go out dancing to my favourite trance or drum n bass DJs alone just because I loved the tunes and would go home again. It was always the music that did it for me, anyway. I never went out because of the drugs; if the music wasn't right, I wasn't interested and wanted to go home. Just ask my friends at the time, HA! I have loved being on my own. And yet, on the timeline convergence on my 38th birthday, it hit me hard, and I didn't think I was going to come back from this one. And yet, somehow, I did.

Your Deepest Fear Is Your Ally.

The things I was most ashamed of became and are my greatest gifts. The gift of being alone has enabled me to get more of my Purpose work done than if I were with someone. I imagine I would've made it happen, but the number of times I have heard clients or other people say how many family and birthday gatherings they have to attend—with 'have' being the operative word—means attendance is also a choice. And yet, it was the thing I most missed when the timeline convergence hit. The level of isolation I have faced and experienced in my life has become the way life is. I have a lot of freedom to do what I want, when I want. My aloneness became my ally. It enabled me to heal deep core wounds and hold a level of strength inside me that many don't ever face in their entire lives.

Shame surfacing at this level of your life is because you're releasing one of the biggest past traumas of your life, which will have deep roots in generational clearing. Not only are you stepping into a new level in your life, but you are breaking the chain right now. This is the turning point where most give up their lives and leave the planet or live a life of bitter resentment and bitterness because they do not have the courage to make life-changing changes! Perhaps they simply do not know how, and that is one huge reason why I train healers in my training school with this specific skill set for this very reason: because society simply needs this level of understanding. So many lives can be saved, let alone the bitterness and resentment released, so people can actually live and lead fulfilling lives instead of being buried under attachment and addiction.

It is important to remember that you might be breaking down and not feeling like you can take another day, let alone another breath. The shame cloak is horrid, and you can't even get out of bed to face the day, let alone open your eyes anymore. It is so important to remember that these are breakthrough points. The darkest night is always just before dawn. The hardest part is always at the end—the part where you want to give up is the hardest, as is when you're about to break through. Just two months after my 38th birthday breakdown, which I thought I could never come back from, my long-time staff member left. It was another blow and a *huge* energetic shift in my business. My other staff member stepped into full-time admin in Reality Awareness. I went from overworking myself and not having time to suddenly having all these tasks that had been bogging me down for ages, suddenly free up and now have all this energetic space. I realised that I had asked the previous member to step in for more hours for years, but she kept saying no. I was 'people-pleaser Hannah' back then and didn't realise that CEO energy says, 'Okay, well, time to go because the business needs a full-time admin now.' Lesson learnt. Another two months later, I had a $25k cash received day in Reality Awareness, taking January 2023 to a $40k month, which was like a Godsend and such a sign that I had broken free from the timeline convergence point four months prior. It was like the timeline convergence point was actually putting me on the right path. I had previously had $40k months in Reality Awareness, but that was from having my signature program open. Yet this came from pure love of what I do—Psychic Readings and working with my Inner Circle clients! 'Do what you love,' they say!

The following month, in February 2023, Reality Awareness hit the $1M mark in all-time revenue. Seven years of literal blood, sweat, and tears and fumbling around, figuring it all out with organic marketing and even figuring out the new system I have been the guardian of, figuring out 'how' I am bringing it to Earth—but not even that, the experiences I had to go through, the initiations, if you will, to be where I am today. Since my full-time admin started in November, I have been cleaning up everything. I didn't realise that, at that time, six years of work were just strewn everywhere. It was an unorganised mess, but I needed to get back in and see how incredible it was. I was in Stephanie Ann Hughson's Collective Membership, and her training brought me back to my truth that year. Even though I was in dire straits, I would always plug into my mentors. They seriously got me to where I am. With my willingness and action-taking, of course! I am ever so grateful for the snippets of incredible 'aha!' moments that helped me clean up everything in my business and life while listening to those trainings.

Ringing and contacting companies where I had unpaid debts, revising the plans so they were more manageable, and taking a break from some for a month or so helped everything become clear again. I was intuitively guided, just at the right time, of course, to YouTube videos of people sharing how they got out of $100k debt by following their God-led plans and taking decisive action, and miracles began happening for them. Well, that did it for me too.

Was it easy? Hell no! It took a while for the shame to be released. But the energetic shifts in my business with the change of staff members and now the full-time admin have made a world of difference. I have tried different staff over the years, but no one tells you that it takes time to find the right person suited to your unique role in this world with your work. Once I began doing what I loved again and just followed that, alongside money tracking, consciously working with my debt, and finding the little snippets of love for my daughter, animals, and what I am good at with my work, when the $25k day came in January that year, I knew I had turned a corner and what I was doing was working—so do more of this, Hannah! The following month was the $1M milestone, and then March saw another $25k day, leaving March with a $50k month. Phew. And yet, just four months before, I was a bawling, howling, eyes-out wreck for months on end, living in overdraft with the biggest timeline convergence point I have ever experienced, contemplating walking away from my business for good because I didn't understand what was happening. Well, I wasn't. I could never. This is what I do. This is my Life Purpose. But I tell you, walking through that fire was insane. I have learnt so much from my seven years of online entrepreneurship, let alone the spiritual walk of fire since my awakening in 2005. Phew, phew, phew! Talk about initiations!

When a timeline convergence point surfaces, you will feel like you're not living your truth. You will feel like everyone can sense it in you and that you've not only done something wrong but that everyone else is succeeding except you. You will feel alone, isolated, and like an outsider like you've never experienced before. You'll want to give it up, seriously consider it, and look into it. What you have to remember here, and this is *crucial*, is that while some timeline convergence points are literally bigger than others, even though they will all feel big in their own right, the reason that this is happening is, of course, to heal from your past, but also that you are about to shift to a major level in your life and have a huge breakthrough. Your life will turn around in ways you cannot even begin to imagine when you are traumatised by the change. When you are in it, it will feel like all your dreams have turned to dust. In manifesting terms, what is actually happening is that they have literally 'disappeared from your dream state'—because they are about to come to Earth, they are in transition. You're about to live them! It is crucial to remember this when you are breaking down. But you won't believe me until after the fact.

The other important factor here is that while we can create our own reality and 'choose not to have big breakdowns' to have a breakthrough and change our life, on certain timeline convergent points, that is what happens! There are layers upon layers of life experiences covering certain core wounds that just can't be breathed away, plant-medicined away, or quantum leapt over. Feeling the depth of consciousness in your Heart is 'how' you truly heal. Nothing can match the healing power of your feeling, healing heart.

While major timeline convergence points are insanely hard, challenging, and deeply emotional times of your life to go through, the more you walk this path of the conscious healer, you will find that after the first 18 months or so, it does get easier. Healing gets easier. You start to know what to expect. The first 18 months, when you begin this healing journey or from the moment you decide to heal from a certain experience in your life, are your hardest days. Some days will be good and high, and others will feel like it all happened yesterday. Know that you are *healing*. Healing is not easy. Nor is it pretty. It is raw. It is emotional. It is hard. It is messy.

Once you've walked this path for a while and have healed huge chunks of your past, it does get easier. You know what to expect. You know how to ride the waves. You know how to ride the rollercoaster when a timeline convergence point is surfacing. The time between healing points (crisis!) becomes longer. Meaning you can enjoy your joy for longer periods! Yay! This is what I would consider 'choosing not to break down to break through'. You can heal through joy instead of pain, and the time between things breaking down and healing gets longer and longer. But you still have to walk through it. Usually, in the beginning, there is a lot of pain to feel because you've had so many years of it built up and buried—until now.

When you're about to step up in your life, you can guarantee there will be some big breakdown or catastrophic event that unfolds—a relationship breakdown, a career change, a health crisis, or something else—maybe a timeline convergence. It can also be the catalyst for a long-overdue change that you have been working on for a long time. Regardless of what it is, there will be some major decisions that you need to make. It is crucial to remember at this point that the decision you make for yourself *is* correct, and after you've made it, you will doubt your decision! Perhaps not in the moment, but in the coming weeks or months, you will question if you made the right decision. I am sure you will come up with good reasons too! It is so important to understand at this point that when 'waves' of this doubt come over you, number 1: keep walking straight through them, and number 2: this is just another wave of grief that is surfacing that you are probably uncomfortable facing and dealing with at this time. Remember, society is trained *not* to feel; however, healing requires that you *do*.

You have definitely made the right decision. No matter how shiny the object of attention is now, you definitely made the right decision. Why? Because it wasn't like at the time you were weighing up the options and thinking, 'Oh, this one feels like the wrong decision; I am going to make this one!' No! You just didn't do that, did you? Sure, people look back in regret; some even go back, but are they happy? Some are sure; however, I guarantee you that if you truly trust yourself on this one, once the hardest part passes, you will move on. You may look back and realise that you've never truly been happy since, but you also know that you left for a reason and that goodness knows what would've happened if you stayed. So, you made the right choice; it is now time to grieve it. And that, as we know, comes in waves and can last for years to come. Be okay with this. Grief is normal. Society is trained to think it is not and that there is something wrong with you; don't listen to society. Listen to your heart. It has important things to share with you. Feel, heal, and eventually, in some way, you will smile again.

When doubt surfaces, know that this is your signal that you have made the right choice and to keep walking forward through it; otherwise, you will keep going back and realising why you left in the first place, and round and round in circles we go. It is why I have my podcast, 'Do I Stay or Do I Go?' It is something I have worked with numerous clients on over the years. No matter if it is a relationship or some other life-changing decision to be made, the work is the same. Do the inner work inside yourself for 30 days, 90 days, or longer, depending on the situation, to get super clear inside yourself before making any decisions. Once the decision is made, back yourself the entire way, no matter who tries to talk you out of it. Listening to your intuition about the decisions you've made, no matter how big or small, will increase your confidence and sense of self. Your life direction will become clear. When you are constantly putting yourself last, listening to everyone but yourself, and staying in situations that are less than your heart's desire, this is the recipe for losing yourself. It is why so many people don't even know what makes them happy anymore or can't make decisions for themselves because they are too busy trying to make everyone else happy or waiting for instructions from the people around them to tell them what to do.

Trusting yourself and the decisions you make requires you to have a strong sense of self. Not everyone is going to agree with you, and not everyone is going to like you. However, you will find your tribe eventually, and there are others that live with integrity and follow their hearts' dreams, too; you have to find them. It is normal when Ancient Blooded Healers step into their Life Purpose for those around them to question, doubt, and put down what they are doing. Some will laugh at you, some will not want to be seen around you, and some will tell you to stop doing what you are doing! WTF! I know! It is insane.

What I found when I began to step up online with Reality Awareness was that it was the ones closest to me that would put me down for what I do! It took me quite some time to realise that when my mother, father, or someone else close to me would say, 'Stop doing this; why are you doing this? Just stop it.' In some way, shape, or form, I realised that because my live streams were public, anyone could see them! That is the basis of 'public' settings, right?

What I realised after a time of questioning what I was doing because those that were closest to me were continually telling me to stop (WTF!) was that they *didn't understand* what I was doing. Now, how do you explain the Universe to someone? It's like explaining what I do. Well, it isn't a simple answer! However, the 'reason' they were telling me to stop this psychic shit is that when I do a public live stream, if they watch it, it then gets shown to all their 'friends' on Facebook, for example. Then that person or friend of theirs watches it and doesn't really understand what I am talking about or why, so the next time they speak with my mother or father and ask them about me, my mother or father gets embarrassed because they don't even know what I do and don't know what to say to their friend. *That* is why they would come to me and say stop because they were embarrassed and didn't know what to say to their friends! Right! #huge

When I realised this, I began to give them ammunition. What I mean by that is, for example, that one day my dad had a 'quiet' chat with me and said that I shouldn't be 'advertising' how much money I have made online in my business. At that time, in early 2019, he referred to a post about my milestone of making $100k in 5 months in my business. It was my biggest milestone at the time, and of course, I am going to celebrate that online! It shows what I do! Of course, I am going to celebrate that. He went on to say he understood, as he was once involved in Nivea skincare years ago, and part of the 'marketing' is sharing how much you are making, so he got it and understood my 'why'. He then went on to say that his mate had seen my post and said to Dad, 'I should ask Hannah for a loan!' And so this was Dad's concern about people knowing how much I was making. I turned around and 'gave Dad ammo', in essence saying, 'Dad, next time someone says something like that, just say to them, "Well, have you sent Hannah a message and asked her?"' Because the reality is that people are too scared to message me, say things, or ask things like that. Now, of course, we both know he wouldn't have (well, he might have!). But he wouldn't have, and he didn't, because watching someone online and actually communicating with them or being in their mentorship is a very different story.

This gave Dad a 'come back' of what to say when people communicate with him like this, rather than just staring blankly and not knowing what to say or being embarrassed or worried. I did something similar with my mum and just told her a few sentences they could say back to their 'friends', asking them about what I did. That way, they could speak clearly about what I did rather than feel silly, stupid, or embarrassed because they didn't know how to respond to questions or explain what I did. Heck, I didn't even know how to describe what I did at the start, and still, today, I sometimes think about how to answer *that* question! I never heard anything after these incidents and was grateful. The funny thing is, after celebrating that milestone, I never heard any of my family tell me not to do this anymore! How about that, hey? It must be working or something! Also, they started to 'see' what I was doing. You can't explain the Universe to someone, but you can show them. Some things are to be felt and experienced, and then conscious understanding comes from this.

Everyone wants to be psychic, but they don't want to tend to deep energetic and traumatic wounds. Everyone wants to be intuitive, but they don't want to feel their emotions to the depths it will take them. Everyone wants to heal, and they try and do so by fasting, going raw vegan, or even being breatharian, but they still wonder why people die on them or that they are on 'the path that keeps you healthy' and wonder why some still end up with cancer and die!

To Be Intuitive, You Must Feel Your Emotions.
To Truly Heal, You Must Feel Your Emotions.

You've just become a master at travelling them. When you work on your intuitive gifts, your trauma will surface. No matter how much work you've done in the past, there are layers of trauma at every level. When you commit to a deep, regular meditation routine, your trauma will surface. When you commit to a strict cleansing diet, your trauma will surface. When you commit to regular yoga classes, your trauma will surface. The reality is that when you do this work, your trauma will surface. The reality of that is that trauma or illness equals buried emotions. The other reality to this, which we have talked about many times here, is that society is trained not to feel. The good news is that you can untrain society's conditioning and train yourself to feel.

Sure, anyone can strengthen their Third Eye through a few meditation practises, but to truly see the truth, an unravelling of all you have ever known, releasing childhood traumas, timeline convergences, and past life inflictions on your intuitive gifts, must be healed. Many people stop or give up their intuitive training because, once the trauma surfaces, they are not taught what to do with it. Many are shown how to strengthen their gifts but not what to do once they open that doorway, and that turns people away, calling it the devil, when it is simply old trauma surfacing that they were not taught what this is. A meditation to increase your Clairvoyance isn't going to heal your deepest childhood trauma unless you are advanced in your skills and know more tools than just a meditation to increase your Clairvoyance. A few mini-courses here and there usually won't bring up the deepest, darkest traumas buried in your psyche, but if you continue on this spiritual healing journey and start feeling off or depressed, I guarantee you it isn't the time to stop. More so, find a specific trauma-healing course (which is what we do in Trust Your Intuition to Become a Certified Intuitive Healer and Life Purpose Activator) and continue with it.

The piece that people miss is that all the meditation, yoga, and connecting to your spiritual guides (or whatever spiritual work you're drawn to and have done to date) has only created a safe foundation *for* the trauma to surface. I also believe that is why some people lose their minds or are tripped into psychosis from plant ceremonies, and why it happens to some people and not others because they do not have this foundational connection to spirit and how to take care of themselves in these situations. This is exactly why I train my Healers the way I do in my course, 'Trust Your Intuition to Become a Certified Healer & Life Purpose Activator', because I have literally had clients come to me and tell me they have ended up in the hospital after a healing session with someone who cut many cords at once and then let her get up and leave. I am astonished, but also not surprised, that this happened. I rarely even cut cords or recommend it because if you don't do it properly, this is what can happen! Aside from it coming back, you don't just cut cords willy-nilly! There is a time and a place for it, but I rarely do it with my clients. I am more about 'let's heal the real reason the cord is there in the first place', then the cord naturally detaches. Any spiritual work involves taking people deep into their psyche. If you do not know what you are doing, don't do it. Train and hone your skills. Work side by side with a trusted healer or someone trained in Reality Awareness. It's like saying you can drive a car, but that doesn't mean you can handle a heavy truck without extra training. Spiritual work and facilitating it are no different.

I encourage you to meditate, attend yoga classes, do what you're guided to do with your spiritual tools and experiences, connect with your angels and spirit guides, or receive messages intuitively. I am all for trusting your intuition about what is right for *you*. But as mentioned, if you start feeling off, depressed, or impatient with it all, it is time to deepen your skills, train, and hone your intuition. You're ready for the next level; that's all. It is definitely not the time to stop but to find the right modality, teacher, and trainer. All the work you've done to date has prepared you for this, and your intuitive gifts are taking you to a clearer, more accurate, and deeply grounded purpose level. And that is to be celebrated!

Strengthening Your Gifts

I will be the first to tell you that if you want to increase your intuition, sitting in long states of meditation on a *regular* basis is required. Not just on a ten-day Vipassana retreat or a 4-day breath work training here and there. I am talking daily for 18 months to 3 years, and let's add in the rest of your lifetime. If you want to advance your skills, this is also what to do, along with many other practises and personal development processes. As you do these things consistently, you become innately tuned in, and that means that in real-time, in everyday life 'off the mat', you will also receive intuition that you can interpret because your skills have increased. That is why learning and honing your intuition is crucial, because your intuition never switches off!

Once our intuition is acquired, we don't *need* to sit in deep states of meditation for long periods of time to hear our intuition speak to us in real time. Remember, your intuition never switches off, but it is the deciphering of your intuition, inner child, shadow part, angels or spirit guides, past lives, or a trauma wound speaking; that is why we pursue the skills that are honed through practise, learning, and personal and psychic development. We have an innate relationship with our intuition and can decipher past-life information and interdimensional information in real time rather than getting stuck trying to figure it out, brushing it off, or thinking you're crazy because someone told you so. No. You build your intuition, you are innately connected to your intuition, you *are* your intuition, and you'll learn to love yourself all over again or for the very first time when you hone your skills in this arena. You discover who you truly are.

It is so important to trust your intuition when information comes in real-time because it will, does, and always has been coming in real-time. It's just now that you're conscious of it and learning the language of your intuition—this most incredible, powerful, and loving relationship you could ever experience on Earth.

You Are Your Intuition.

As you strengthen and activate your unique intuitive gift, you learn 'how' it is part of you on a day-to-day basis. So many people are 'doing their intuition' before you even realise you're 'doing your intuition'. It is not like a dawning lightbulb moment of clarity of thought. You could be making bone broth soup and adding dried mushrooms and realise how in tune and in alignment that is for your body's constitution in the middle of winter, and yet you didn't know this until after the fact. Someone randomly started telling you all the Chinese, Ayurvedic, and Nourishing Traditions' healing properties suddenly, out of nowhere, and it gives you confirmation of what you were doing last week in the kitchen, and it was exactly what your body needed! *That*'s 'Doing Your Intuition' before you're conscious of it. This is definitely the trait of an Ancient Blooded Healer. We are innately connected to the flow of intuition that *is within* us.

You Are Your Intuition.

It is why many people 'freak out' when they are around us. They wonder how we 'just knew' certain things or that you don't set a timer when cooking because you 'just know' when your food is ready. Maybe you freak out because you 'forgot about the food'! But then you run to the kitchen time and time again and realise it is just right and ready, not burned! You start to realise that your intuition was telling you it was ready! You Are Your Intuition. Every part of you is your intuition. Sure, there is your Claircognisence, Clairvoyance, Clairaudience, Clairsentience, and a zillion different chakras and other portals on your body that you can hone, activate, learn about, and go deeper into. But the reality is that *You Are Your Intuition*. The entirety of you is your intuition. Everything you do, everything you think, everything you say—it's all your intuition. Why? Because it is you! You are in a human body, sure, but that body is only alive because your consciousness is in your body! And your consciousness is connected to your intuition; it is your intuition that makes your body function. The more you can lean into the trust that everything you say, do, and are is your intuition, the more you become a living, walking beacon of intuition that is magic, lights up the world, and illuminates your path with blessings. You become intuitively stronger; you hear more, see more, and can live in the fullness of what you are here to be—YOU.

Sound and Music are Everything to You.

Ancient Blooded Healers are deeply connected to music. Music is everything, and music is life. We listen to music in everything we do, and we always have something playing in our ears or in the background. Perhaps it is a training, a podcast, an audiobook, or music—something is always playing, or you're creating it. This can be a trauma wound in that we always need something in the background or on because if there was just silence, that would bring up feelings we are not ready to face. However, music is deeply connected to Clairaudience. Sound, what you hear, the messages in sounds, the lyrics that speak to you, the words behind the words. You are going along minding your business—shopping, for example—and suddenly it is like all you can hear on the speaker in the shop is the song, the lyrics so clear to you, reminding you of your dad and a message to call him. If he has passed away, he is reaching out to you, reminding you that he is right by your side. It is as if all the shop noises drown out, and like a megaphone beaming just the sound of the song, it comes so clearly to your ears that it stops you in your tracks as you truly 'hear the message' of this clairaudient moment.

Your Ears. It is related to the colour magenta. It is where we hear messages. It is your Clairaudience. It is why I teach with eight chakras, not seven. Our Clairaudience is a part of our intuition. Truth be told, we have thousands of chakras in our bodies. However, I focus on the eight in my teachings. We have two ears for a reason; they look like ovaries and relate to fertility, the feminine, and openness. Something that has been shunned from society over the millennia, and witches were burned at the stake to 'get rid of the magic'. The Eight Chakras bring back balance to humanity, not the inverted, upside-down, distorted, and unbalanced seven. Sure, this is just a perspective, and everyone resonates differently. However, I also know it is a huge part of my purpose to bring back this awareness of eight, the balance, and the divine feminine. Eight is a balanced number, and seven is an odd number. It is also why I teach from the Crown Chakra down to the Base Chakra, as we have been 'reaching up to Heaven' for too long when Heaven is inside of us. We need to be grounded in our body to even hear our intuition, let alone channel that to 'Earth' through our Base Chakra. You take those brilliant ideas (Crown Chakra), see the truth of them (Third Eye), hear the deep understanding of your mission (Ear Chakras), speak and live that truth into fruition (Throat Chakra), live from your heart in all that you do and do it with love (Heart Chakra), come into purposeful alignment of your Soul's Mission with your true balanced power, leave situations that are not in alignment with your Soul (Solar Plexus), gestate those creations (Sacral Chakra/Womb) until their fruition, and birthing them to Earth (Base Chakra)—the true dedication of your Life Purpose.

As an Ancient Blooded Healer, music speaks to you. You will be going through a rough patch in your life, and your favourite DJ or band will bring out a new track whose lyrics explain exactly what you're going through, and it will get you through. It is like the greatest saviour to you ever because no one else is there for you, but this music is. You feel something so much deeper, speaking to you, there for you, like it was made just for you. That Spirit has your back even in the hardest times when it feels like you have absolutely no one, and most of the time, you don't.

This is the connection with your Clairaudience. That deep feeling that accompanies what you 'hear' in the music—something so much deeper than just the words, lyrics, or melody—is all of that at the same time. It is like you 'read' the music so much deeper than anyone else who 'just listens to it'. You hear the architecture of sound. You've even had people look at you weirdly when you try to explain the music, so you just don't anymore. You've also had people ask you why you *always* have music on or in your ears or something!

The quality of the sound has always been important to you. I was always so pedantic about the sound quality, the bass depth, and all the pieces. It is definitely important! I used to be the one sitting against the huge bass subwoofer speakers at raves and festivals, right up front, ear to ear with the speaker. The bass would take me somewhere. It would shift something out of me. Not that I knew it at the time, but the bass is everything. Sound is everything. Music is everything. It takes me somewhere. It connects me. To Spirit, to Source, to my Spirit, to my intuition, to the flow of life, and to all that is. Music is creation.

God said, 'Let there be Light'.

But there had to be Sound to make those words of Light. *Right?*

That one.

Sound is Creation.

I would always have to have music going, no matter what I was doing. However, when I healed my deepest mother and father wounds, I found that the way I was so pedantic about music—the quality, the constant need for it—shifted. I didn't 'need' that anymore. I was okay in silence. I was okay hearing Life. I was okay being present with myself. It reminded me a bit of when I stopped smoking weed. I began when I was 13 years old and smoked it every day until I was 21. When I was 21 and had my spiritual awakening through a heavy relationship breakup in the middle of my stint of hard-core recreational drug-taking years prior (2005), I started my year-long training in spiritual and psychic development that set me on the path of what I still live, breathe, and teach today. This naturally took me off the 'need' for drugs, especially when I learnt about them in depth in the training when it went into what they do to your psyche and aura. I didn't want that! I began to slowly ease off the weed. I began only having it on the weekends. Then, eventually, it was just at festivals. Then, nine months later (that's nine months again!), I stopped it completely. I didn't need it. I didn't want it. But the part about the 'need' is that I found that reality—Life—wasn't that bad after all! Of course, I had done a tonne of healing work through the year-long psychic development training at that time, but I became okay in reality because I healed.

Music has been the same. With the constant need for it to always be there, I began to be okay with being present with myself again. Which is what I was good at when I gave up drugs back in 2006. However, when I found out I was unexpectedly pregnant in 2008, my entire world changed, and music became my saviour—specifically, Yoga and Kundalini Chants. Yoga was my saviour through my pregnancy, training as a yoga teacher at the same time, and raising my daughter on my own. More on that story at another time.

Your Clairaudience 'speaks' to you. You hear the lyrics behind the lyrics; you hear what people are not saying; you hear the slightest sounds and movements because you're picking up the vibrations with the feathers on your arms and your nervous system. You hear what animals and trees are saying and what the realms are saying. You are clear on what the different voices are in your head. If you're not, after reading this book, you're ready to study and get clear on it because you definitely have a zillion thoughts running through your head per second or millisecond, know that you hear so deeply, and wonder why no one else hears what you do.

You Are Gifted.

You understand the depth of the lyrics in songs. It is like you hear what the musician was going through when they created that song. You feel it. You hear it. You understand it, could pick it apart better than anyone you know, and would be on point with its meaning. Isn't that normal? For you, dear Ancient

Blooded Healer, and for us, it is. Your Clairaudience is strong. You are very vocal, and you voice almost everything you hear. You chant, sing, and hum frequently, and you have always been told your voice is soothing and that people could listen to you for hours. Not only do you hear it, you feel it. You can be listening to something and then feel like eating a particular food because the musician just ate that food or was eating it while creating that music! Not that you would have confirmation of that physically, but you intuitively just know stuff like that.

You've always known stuff. Your sense of knowing is ridiculously on point, and you always say things and are like, 'Well, isn't that normal? Why didn't they think of that way of doing things?' You're an Ancient Blooded Healer, and this is your gift. Many Ancient Blooded Healers are highly Claircognisent. You just know things: you know when the food is ready, you know who is calling or messaging before you look at the phone, you know what people in the household are going to say before they say it, you know what the driver in front of you is going to do before they do it—you just know things. This sometimes freaks people out, but you don't even think about it; you just know things. You get those brilliant ideas out of the blue, and you think like a lightning bolt with ideas and thoughts that most people have difficulty keeping up with you. It is so important to Master this gift of yours. It allows you to function in society as well as hold the depth of gift that you have to support humanity with the reason you were born.

Doreen Virtue coined the term many years ago, and it felt so on point to me: ADHD is Attention Dialled into a Higher Dimension. It is so on point. Super tapped into and dialled into a higher dimension. Many mental illnesses stem from someone not being grounded in their body. The flip side to this is that when they do come into their body, they feel. Society is trained not to feel, so they are told something is wrong with them, and around the vicious cycle we go. Physical ailments in the body are caused by trauma of some sort, which causes a person to disassociate with their body. They do not feel safe, so they excarnate out of the body, and the Soul lingers just above the body. They then find coping mechanisms to deal with society on a daily basis. These people can be super tapped into Spirit, but they are very ungrounded and frequently get told the lights are on but no one is home, or worse, that they are crazy. As I have mentioned, the buildup of stored emotions from the event that one is 'not allowed to feel' piles up upon each other like scar layers. Many people struggle to cry, and it is because of these scar layers that they need to be peeled back, like the ice layers melting, before tears start to fall. It is why you may have heard the term 'layers of the onion'. You keep uncovering wounds and traumas when you heal. Yes, you do, unless you go straight to the core and unravel from there, which is what I train you to do in my Trust Your Intuition to Become a Certified Intuitive Healer and Life Purpose Activator Course. When you go straight to the core, all the layers may dissolve and be 'irrelevant' to go into, or only the ones that remain important for whatever reason are important to work with consciously in healing.

These scar layers can be focused on a particular area of the body or be all over the body. It is why awesome metaphysical manuals have been published, connecting emotions with ailments in the body and explaining what original thought patterns created them. That, layered upon the scar tissue of events to date and the coping mechanisms that are currently present for a person to be dealing with societal pressures, allows for one big recipe for an intricate puzzle that no one seems to understand, figure out, piece together, or care to. And yet, it is the epitome of true healing. It is why I am passionate about what I teach, live, and preach: for this very reason, this information *must* be made available if society is to truly heal!

Ancient Blooded Healers tend to have a gift for cutting straight to the truth. We smell bullshit miles away, and with training, your skills become tenfold better at piecing all the puzzle pieces together and immediately seeing the truth of the dynamics. We ask *why* about everything. We were often one of those kids who asked why about everything and asked why some more. Still today, our brain goes into auto mode, figuring out why and asking more whys. This is *why* you are so gifted; do not ever change your 'asking why'.

When our skills are not trained and we are 'hovering just above our body', we can be sharp with our words, seem cold, not explain things, say 'weird things' that people don't understand, and even be scared to tell the whole truth. So you play around with words, and people think you're strange because you talk strangely. Truth be told, you probably don't even know how to explain what you're sensing, decipher what you're picking up intuitively, or even how to say to the person what you're intuitively sensing! Sometimes, in this instance, you may be a person who doesn't speak up, and then things get worse, and you wish you had said something!

Dear Ancient Blooded Healer, it is time for you to heal, step up, and hone your skills. You're highly tapped in for a reason; you sense there is something greater than you; you're here to do something, and it will constantly gnaw away at you no matter how much you try and drown it out with your addiction of choice—it just won't work. It will always be there, tapping you on the shoulder, awaiting you to say, 'OKAY, IT'S TIME!'

Chapter 7

Different Fears That Halt Your Life Purpose

Have you ever had that feeling of leaving home and having to turn back because you think you left the stove on and have to make sure that it is off because you don't want to burn the house down? It is so ridiculously strong, and yet, you also know deep down you didn't leave it on, but you don't trust yourself; you are usually stressed out anyway, and the thought of your house burning down is just... 'No, I have to turn back and check'. 99.9% of the time, if not all the time, you didn't leave it on, but the fear is so strong that it makes you run later than you already are, it peaks the stress levels and you just don't need this, especially today! What about the feeling that you have forgotten something? Or that you haven't locked the door or something? Something that makes you go back! Usually more than just once!

Take note. When you feel this strongly, it is also only at particular times in your life, right? It isn't ALL the time. Not every single time, every single day, all the time, forever, right? No. So, when you feel this and are in a 'phase' of it, there are two things here.

Number 1: You're going through a very stressful phase in your life. You can also be at a timeline convergence point at the same time, which only accentuates the stress and feelings associated with this.

Number 2: This fear of the house burning down comes from being burned at the stake as a witch. You'll find that in these phases of your life, you are either doing something out of alignment with your Soul, being wrongly accused, or breaking through to a new level in your business or life. The fear is so strong because, in a past life, you *were* killed at this point in your life, just when you were about to succeed or were succeeding at what you do best.

For example, if you are staying in a relationship that you know deep down is not in your best interest and your intuition is guiding you to leave, but you're not listening. Being out of alignment with your intuition will make you flighty and anxious, move you into depression (suppression of Soul), and eventually make you gain weight, get sick, or do both. This will set your nervous system on high alert, so the fear of your house burning down – or that you have forgotten something - is a sign that you are not on the right path and that something is deeply out of alignment. It can even mean that you simply need a break! A break will definitely calm your nervous system. However, if that doesn't do it, the wrongly accused is your next check-in and port of call here.

'Wrongly accused' can be when you're in a situation where you're stepping into your Life Purpose work and/or up-levelling to your next phase, and all these people seem to come out of the woodwork and tell you why you shouldn't be doing what you're doing (simply because they do not understand!). In a past life, it is very common to harbour wounds from when you were burned at the stake, hung, or killed in some way for simply living your life—your Life Purpose—which is showing up in present-day reality when you feel this. The majority of people hit a 'freeze' wound in moving forward in their Life Purpose work at some point, as their body, muscle, and soul memory are going, 'Yeah, no, I was killed last time at this point; I am not moving forward with this, thanks!' It is your survival instinct to keep living; there is nothing wrong with that at all! Just keeping you alive here! However, it is the current day and age, not your past life anymore. It is safe to move forward in this life doing what you're doing; however, your body, muscles, and soul memory won't let you! It can show up as sabotage in some way, shape, or form. You can use my Healing from the Witch Hunts Meditation to instantly release this fear/freeze and trauma, so you can move forward again without being halted by it.

When there is a fear of the world collapsing all around you, whether through current world events like a food shortage or some other world event, it is a deep and usually quite large childhood trauma of neglect. It will be all the times as a child that you were neglected, that you needed your mother, father, or family in some way, shape, or form, and it will be layered in what I call the 'scar tissue layers' of this wound. Usually, between 36 and 50 years of age, it can be rife and 'run your life' if you are not conscious and tending to this wound. It will be all you talk about, and you'll spend most of the time running on adrenaline out of fear that you're going to run out or the world is going to fall apart. Reality check: there is an abundance of wealth, food, and resources in every country. Sure, there are some places of extreme poverty too, but the reality is that there are both. You could get on a plane, go to Dubai, and experience opulence instantly. The fear of the world collapsing around you is your own world collapsing around you, meaning the trauma and grief of this wound surfacing would completely change your world and the trajectory of your life if you faced it.

If you look through the threads carefully, a fear of no food in the world results from emotional neglect as a child and not being emotionally nourished as a child. But somehow, as a child, food was always on the table (mostly). This wound shows up today for you as a food shortage because food is how you learnt to receive the emotional nourishment you lacked as a child. So a lack of food today would trigger so deeply the lack of emotional nourishment you actually received as a child. To run out of food would mean facing the grief of this wound, which is not bearable, so it is better to focus on food instead. This can be compounded by the loss of relationships over the years because, again, the emotional loss of the love that you started to receive as an adult and that you didn't get as a child is also 'taken away' from you, whether through a breakup, divorce, death, or some other major event. It will trigger emotional neglect and emotional starvation wounds from your childhood. Here, this 'no food/food shortage fear' would be a 'scar layer' on the original wounding.

When there is a fear of a tsunami 'on its way', there is literally a tsunami of change about to 'hit that person's life'. They are literally feeling the immense change on their doorstep. They might pack their house up into storage, get in their car, or get on a plane and leave the area. They may or may not know where they are going, but they know they cannot stay. Sometimes it is out of this fear of the tsunami coming; other times, it is just an immense emotion of change that they are feeling. They may have come to the realisation that they cannot continue in the long-term relationship that they have been in.

This is the collapse of the old paradigm structure of their lives that they have been living to date. This is the tsunami of change they are feeling. The loss of this relationship may uncover the original wound of the loss of family, which is the biggest wound one can face and definitely feels like a tsunami's worth of grief! No wonder one wants to pack up everything and get away!

When people fear AI taking over the world, obsess over robots, and try to determine if we're living in a simulation or not, it triggers deep-seated abandonment and betrayal wounds related to the mother and father figures. Typically, within the next 2–3 years, these wounds will reach their 'pinnacle', deeply resurfacing and causing what feels like the biggest dark night of the Soul they've ever experienced. It will be the biggest breakdown they've ever had, feeling like death to their soul and world. However, this is also the biggest breakthrough they can experience in changing their reality, even though it won't feel like it at the time. It may start with a relationship breakup of some kind, and no matter how many cord-cutting candle rituals they do, nothing helps except feeling the grief of it. The one thing many humans avoid is feeling.

No amount of plant medicine, psychedelic sitting journeying, chanting, humming, breath work, or ice plunges can avoid the real work of feeling your own damn heart and the grief that is trying to come out and sending you insanely crazy—you will literally feel like you're losing your mind. The AI fears triggers this, as with the core wounds of mother and father surfacing from deep below; the healing of these wounds at the core level is what literally changes your mental wiring and your cellular structure and is always triggered by a particular relationship that was a 'replacement for one of these parents'. You will find similar patterns in either your mother or father, or both, in correlation to the relationship you are desperately trying to let go of but can't, no matter what you do.

The AI fear is the 'technology' of your brain that you are scared of. Meaning, when you heal the mother and father core wounds, which can surface at different layers of your life but are very common around the 36–42 years of a person's life, the technology is activating in your own self. Healing mother and father core wounds is your anchor to this earth. Without your mother and father, who are you? You may not even speak to them, but they still energetically rule your life. The mother and father are the core anchors that keep you grounded and anchored, and here on this Earth plane, they created and brought you here (so to speak). When this core wounding is surfacing to heal, it is plugging into a new source. Meaning, when you unplug from your parents and the family system and heal the mother and father wounds (and there are always layers), what is left? Without plugging into your mother and father energetically, all you have is you and Source. That is scary for some.

This is why AI fear becomes strong for a person at this time. Without the family system plug or a strong, solid connection to Source, the little boy and little girl inside of them are experiencing their entire energetic world collapsing around them. Whether a person loves or hates AI, whether they are obsessed with it or are scared of how robots are going to rule our world. (#realitycheck, they already do, plus, it is the next industrial revolution. We've had many of these 'resets' of industrial revolutions over the centuries and beyond! 'Hey, Siri!' 'Hey, Alexa!' Cruise control of your car, anyone? Mobile phones themselves— I could go on. We've been in it for a long time, in subtle ways and in ways we haven't even been aware of.)

When I delved into this AI fear, I was fascinated by people being scared of, obsessed with, and worried about adrenochrome. Hey, let's be real; we should be! Whatever you believe on these subjects is irrelevant to the fact that human trafficking is no joke. It is very real and, of course, hidden from the mainstream world. I believe that is changing 100%, but when I was shown many things from this 'dark world', my favourite question was, 'Why?' Why, why, WHY? It is so natural for me to ask this question; it takes me to the core of the wound, to the reason, to the *why*. You know how we Ancient Blooded Healers just get to the core issues right away and are like, 'Um, isn't this normal?' That one.

Anyway, I was asking why a lot, and eventually, it came to me. They are trying to 'eat the Source', but more so, connect to the Source to be a part of it. They even 'showed it' in Avatar: The Way of the Water when they chased the whales and took one tiny part from them (it broke my heart seeing that!), but what and why are they doing it? It angered me, to say the least—why don't they connect to their own Source? Everyone can, and everyone has the capabilities to do this, even though some will 'argue' that with me saying that the 'reptiles' can't, but the reality is that we ALL come from the same Source!

Dark and Light are no separation too big for God! Source! Universe! Consciousness! Whatever label you want to put on it, we all come from the same place! *That* is reality! I don't believe there is one big man sitting up in heaven, but I do believe there is something bigger than us that connects us all together and that we all come from and return to—Consciousness. We *are* Consciousness. What is interesting to me is that no matter what, any human from any religion, sector, or country on Earth believes 'their god is *the* God'. Yet what is fascinating is that all religions lead back to the One and Only God. Imagine if everyone could just agree that there is something that no one can actually label. That it is too big of a comprehension beyond what our human minds can conceive, let alone what humans have been trained to believe, so we 'don't figure it out or know the truth of'. Never mind that if we did understand it, the reality is that we more than likely wouldn't be in this realm anymore.

They say that The Matrix is a documentary. I believe the same about the Avatar movies; let's extend that to any movie or show. It takes stealing from each other's Source to a whole new level when we understand that 'everyone is plugged into each other instead of Source, sometimes in unhealthy, toxic, unethical, and immoral ways. For a long time, I kept asking my famous question of 'why' about how they say that when we watch movies, Netflix, or anything else, it is 'us giving them permission to do what they do'. I was like, 'What?' I understood it, but I didn't. Then, as time went on with that very important question, *'why'*, it dropped in.

Anything we focus our attention on grows, consciously manifesting itself. This is the law; we know this! Wherever your attention goes, energy flows. Yes? We live in an infinite, universal realm where we can create anything we want, including other realms and worlds. Whatever one you give your attention to, it grows! Hence, all the things you watch *become* worlds. Your energy is pouring into it simply because you are watching it, observing it, or immersed in it. This made me realise 'why' 'they' have created things like Hollywood—to create worlds beyond worlds and more. Let alone if one can 'read between the lines', one is shown a lot of truths. Because it won't be the whole truth—no, don't give it all away and keep them confused! Typical and clever narcissistic trait to keep power energy feeding from the host, right?

That is why, in the Ear Chakra Consciousness, it became so clear about the realms, and a very big part of this Ear Chakra Consciousness is the different realms. In 2020, I did an incredible live stream on the Crown Chakra Consciousness, as I always channel fresh whatever wants to be spoken about with each Chakra when we do the Chakra Consciousness Journey. It was here that it came through so strongly about 'stealing from each other's Source' instead of connecting to their own Source. This applies to any unhealthy relationship, no matter the 'level' of the relationship, whether parent-child, partner, society-government, or any other relationship. A healthy relationship is one where someone has their own connection with their own Source. I am not talking about just God. I am talking about healthy interdependence in the relationship. When both parties are connected to themselves, their own intuition, and their own lives *in* the relationship, there is no need to 'steal' energy or life force from each other because each is connected to their own Source. Hence 'why' those doing that 'to the children' on our Earth are simply too scared to connect to their own Source. Standing in your power, holding your ground, living, speaking, and standing up for the truth require you to be connected to your own Source.

It is why I would get so frustrated (at times!) when, especially during the 2020 wave, people would go around calling people asleep and sheeple. Like seriously? Do you not realise that

1. Your judgement of them keeps them stuck there, and
2. they simply haven't woken up yet and don't know how to connect to their own Source. #simple
3. I shouldn't need to say it, but for the sake of reminders, you can't force someone awake. It is an experience they go through. No matter how much you force information on someone, they will never get it to the depth required for true change. That can only come from someone's internal state and own timelines. Instead of calling them names, which has no different energy vibration than the one you are trying to wake them up from (pot calling the kettle black!), you're better off living your Life instead of shaking people by the arms, screaming in their faces, and trying to explain shit to them they won't understand! Write a book or blog, or get on a live stream instead. You won't look like a crazy person running around like a headless chook! And you might find your *actual* Purpose in the process. Those running around calling them asleep and sheeple are just as scared of their own Power as they are of those scared of what the government is doing to us. In July 2018, I wrote a blog that I shared on social media that explains this perfectly:

The truth about why you are so angry, frustrated, and ultimately scared of what the government is doing?

They seem to have a lot of power and control.

And right there is your KEY.

You are angry because under all anger is sadness.

Sadness that they are hurting people on the planet. Their own fellow kind.

And you just wish that they would just wake the f*%k up already.

I see you. I see you so angry and frustrated, and at the core of this is absolute powerlessness about what to do.

Yes, people have written books and movies on the 'world order' and what is coming.

Maybe it is.

Maybe it isn't.

Why the maybes?

Because, honey, NOTHING IS SET IN STONE.

Honey, all of our tomorrows are created by the choices, actions, and thoughts we make, think, say, be, and act on today. That is how tomorrow is created, which is how we create our future.

Come on.

If you are aware, spiritual, and conscious of 'what they are doing' and are feeling what I am writing or getting agitated and angry at me because 'I am not seeing what THEY are doing', honey, it is just where you are at.

There are three levels of awakening. Actually, there is more, but let me keep it simple for you this second.

1. Unconsciousness

2. Waking up—angry, lost, confused, powerless—wondering what the f&*k is wrong with the world and 'why can't they see what they are doing to them!'
3. Coming into LOVE

If you are conscious and aware, you see the truth through the illusion they hold over the unconscious people who have yet to wake up, yes?

100% f*&king yes, you do.

Good.

So, now that you are awake, honey, you have a deep responsibility.

To yourself, your life, humanity, and the planet.

If you are awake and conscious, you believe you create your own reality on some level, yes?

And the anger and frustration that come are that, well, I didn't create this blah blah blah; it's 'them'.

Honey, if you believe you create your own reality and believe that the Universe IS IN YOU and out there is an illusion, then how is it THEM?

The tricky part is finding the delicate balance, isn't it?

And part of the frustration is trying to understand: if this is all an illusion, then why the f*%k is this going on, and people are feeling pain, dying, getting hurt, being poisoned, being brainwashed, and the list is endless? I am sure you could name a zillion other things.

Yes, it isn't about ignoring it.

But, honey, if you are awake and conscious, you should know the truth.

The substance that woke you up—what was that?

That—what you are focusing on most of the time is what comes into your reality—is the energy you are feeding the energy that grows, correct?

Didn't you learn that your thoughts are creating your reality?

Didn't you learn that your thoughts are creating your feelings, which are creating your reality?

'But what about THEM? THEY are doing this; I didn't create this in my reality. I am all peace and love'. I hear you say.

Are you? So you don't have ANY other emotions in you but peace and love ALL the time? Pfft! We are humans, beautiful! Even I get very angry!

Honey, if you are creating your reality...

If your thoughts are creating...

And if the Universe is IN you, if you are the Universe...

Then how can it be THEM?

This?

This is your next level of consciousness.

Awakening to the truth of the illusion and what 'they' are doing is the first wake-up, yes.

Then, it is up to you to do something about it because now that you are awake, you sure can't go back to sleep, as much as I bet you sometimes wish you could.

So what do you do about it?

This moves into Shadow Work.

This is your next level of consciousness.

This is what transforms the planet.

Yes, don't ignore it.

But don't feed it, either.

If it is in your awareness, if you are feeling strongly about it, if you are pissed off, angry, frustrated at THEM, and just wish people would wake up to the truth already, and underneath all that is because you feel powerless at what to do, honey, this is your calling card that you are ready for the next level of consciousness—Shadow Work.

This is integrating the darkest parts of humanity.

All the hurt, suffering, pain, and more you are seeing in the world and feeling so darn passionate (angry passionate about changing some bloody how), you are ready to integrate these parts of darkness of humanity that are a reflection of yourself because the Universe is you because your thoughts are projecting into the world what you are. YOU, honey, are made up of everything that this Universe is, right?

You are oneness.

You are love at your core, yes?

This is what you teach, correct?

If you are awake and conscious, you teach this on some level.

That we are love, connect into oneness, breathe—OM... yes?

So, honey, this means the darkness too.

This means the hurt and suffering.

Because if you are oneness, how are you separate from that?

The answer to 'how' you can wake those up is to integrate, through Shadow Work, exactly what you are seeing in your reality.

It is the surest and fastest way to wake them up.

Why?

Because when you integrate it through Shadow Work (and this goes for ANYTHING you are agitated about in your reality), you don't have the same charge about that thing anymore.

And what happens then?

You return to the Love, Compassion, and Peace that you are.

And then what happens?

Because you have returned to the true essence of who you are, LOVE

You tap into an infinite resource for creative solutions on how to solve the 'problem' that you see in the world.

YOU become the change in the world because you are that—you are not separate from the hatred in the world.

Remember, if it is in your awareness, you are ready for integration. You are ready for the next level of conscious evolution in your life, which shifts the planet into the next level of consciousness, and you return the Planet and Humanity to that consciousness of Love.

And if you are not integrating, through Shadow Work, the darkness you are seeing in the world (the hate, fear, hurt, pain, lies, and deception), then you are not doing your job as a conscious and aware soul! The truth is love, and in Love, there is no hate. It dissolves. When you turn a light on in a dark room, the darkness is transformed.

Debbie Ford brought huge awareness of Shadow Work to the planet, and I am sure there are others too.

Do you understand why you are so frustrated with the government?

Because, honey, the power you see they have over the world (apparently, isn't that an illusion because everything 'out there' is an illusion?)

The truth?

The truth is that you are conscious and awake because you are powerful beyond measure.

And you are hating on the government because of how powerful they are—are you hating on yourself because, actually, you are that f*&king powerful? You are so scared of reclaiming that truth and using it to benefit humanity, which is ultimately what you want to do, but the thing we want the most is what we are so scared of.

As Marianne Williamson says, 'It isn't our darkness we are afraid of; it is our Light'.

Reclaim your power.

Because if you don't, you are projecting how powerful you really are onto the government, and that keeps them in control until you take back your power, dear powerful, awake, conscious soul.

Reclaim your power and teach others to do the same.

Your most powerful tool is your energy.

Use it wisely.

Claim it.

Own it, powerful Lightworker.

Stand in it, dear Ancient Blooded Healer.

I see you.

Create your own reality. All of it. You DO have this power.

YOU ARE THE UNIVERSE, REMEMBER?

Love, Hannah The Life Purpose Queen

It would always fascinate me on the majority of my live streams on Facebook that would start gaining traction and virility that I would get a wave of comments, mostly abuse, and then a pile of private messages saying that I need to stop this crap, that I am the devil, and that I must turn to Jesus! **cues eye roll!**

Now, I have nothing against what anyone believes! I am the *first* to tell you to trust your intuition about what feels right for you! *This* is what I live, teach, and preach! But when I get a wave of people coming and telling me how to live my life and what to believe in, it turns me away faster than anything. My Inner Rebel loves being told what to do! #not

My take on Jesus is that 'He' is a Consciousness, and 'Jesus returning' is a Consciousness Awakening, which you can feel a huge wave of strongly every Easter. However, I felt it most strongly at Easter 2017, and I believe this is 'when' His Consciousness most flooded and activated the planet *via* consciousness. I saw a post not long ago on Facebook by a dear friend, and he shared how if Jesus really did physically return, most believers would be ranting and raving, 'DEVIL!' It made me laugh at that reality—how true it would be! Who would truly not freak out if Jesus came back to life and walked around again? Anyway, I could go on.

It is important to understand that when any human being tries to control or force an opinion on another human being, whether consciously or unconsciously, deep underneath, they are simply *scared*.

Sacred they are going to be abandoned.

Scared they are going to lose power.

Scared they are going to lose adoration.

Scared they are going to lose love.

Scared their entire reality will fall apart.

Scared of change.

Scared.

Why?

Because underneath, deep down, as kids, they did not receive the love, care, and validation they needed!

This does not excuse controlling or abusive behaviour—nope! Not at all.

But it gives your super-strong-willed analytical mind the answer to WHY.

When you understand this, it drops the judgement.

When you understand this, there is no need to gossip about them. (Oh, and by the way, if you are gossiping about them or spreading all the blogs and podcasts about them, you are simply wounded at your core by what 'they currently did to you' and, deeper than that, by your own mother and father wounds'.)

Now, people will probably come at me and say that this is their purpose (to talk about world stuff) and that what I am saying is 'wrong' (about their purpose). Well, you just proved my point.

When you understand your mission, you carry on with your Purpose.

When you understand your Purpose, you are able to focus on your own mission.

When you understand that the focus and dedication to your purpose 100% doesn't involve a fabric of reality that is tearing down what someone else is doing—no, because you're too focused on building new systems and structures on our planet because you understand the flow, because you understand what is needed, because you are solution-focused because you are so excited about the solution to the problem and you're building it either on your own, building your farm, or building an empire—no matter who calls you crazy, this is what you're doing because well, how can you not see this is the solution? Not feeding the problem with your negative bullshit!

But remember:

When someone is negative, it is because they are hurting, and most times, they are unconscious of their hurting. It is too painful to look within, so they project.

Again, this does not excuse the behaviour, nor does it excuse abuse—none of that.

But now you understand.

And perhaps even in your own life.

You can be so happy and carefree while doing your creative, changing-the-world thing.

And then, over time, you can get bogged down. Hurt. Abandoned by those you love the most and thought they were actually excited for you. Suddenly, the betrayal hits you like a tonne of bricks. And you shut down. Get depressed. Wondering, 'WTF just happened?' And start to be so negative and hurting that you don't even realise it until one day, BAM! Something wakes you the fuck up. You hit a brick wall. All your creativity has gone. Nothing comes out. Caput. Empty. Gone. Burnt out. What. The. Actual. Fuck.

Focusing on what others are doing, whether past family, past lovers, past mentors, or governments, is because you are hurting from losses in your own life. Somewhere along the timeline of your own life, you *have not healed*. Focusing on what the government is doing or what they did to you, is also a level of healing.

Let me explain.

Healing involves

1. Awareness
2. Healing
3. Move on

In simple terms.

But anyone who 'tries to heal' knows that it ain't simple and doesn't feel good, let alone that there is no road map to healing, which is why society is like it is!

Healing looks something like this:

1. *Awareness* Waking up to the reality of what really happened. Shock. Disbelief. Not sure what to do with that information. Anger. Frustration. Grief. Life can fall apart here. Life gets stuck here. Your life becomes a mess. You fall apart. Perhaps your life shatters and destroys from what it always was. You start to throw judgements at others out of anger and fear, saying, 'But this is what they are doing to us!' The reality is that there are people doing bad things to people on this planet. Let's be real. And yet, many people get stuck here because they neither understand nor know how to heal it! And really, the healing can be so simple (in a way), but society is taught that something is wrong with them for feeling and to go and get a pill instead. Of course, many are waking up, but many still don't know how to truly heal the core wounds that change everything. It is here that we move to step #2, healing.

2. *Healing is* messy. Healing takes a long time. It can take anywhere from 18 months to 3 years to truly change a cycle, pattern, or deep trauma, depending on what you're dealing with. When you have a 'whole package of healing', like what I do working with my clients, that heals trauma, teaches the client how to heal themselves at the same time, and steps them on to and accelerates their Life Purpose, I will be honest when I say it takes a good 18 months to 3 years for that effect to truly shift in their reality. Yes, things can shift in rapid time, but time and time again over the many years I have been living and breathing this career, I see it time and time again—18 months to 3 years. 18 months feels like a slog, like hard work, like nothing is working or any change or momentum has been made at all. Yet, deep down, there has definitely been a big change, but your external reality is mostly the same. The internal hasn't quite rippled out to the external yet. Then at the 9-month mark, a 'pop', a little change of some kind, usually a lot of anger, resentment, and

deep hurt surfaces. You can feel good, but not good. At 18 months, like a breath of fresh air, you definitely notice a change! Things start shifting, even though they are still very hard, if not harder than they were before, but you definitely feel and experience a change in your reality. Then at 3 years, CHANGE. You've popped through a bubble; you've broken through a glass ceiling you thought you'd never shift. Phew! Things 'could' and probably are easier, but your training wheels are still on this new reality that you've been working so hard to break through to, whether in healing, business, or any other endeavour. You could receive more kickbacks from people you thought would support you than you've ever had before, making you question EVERYTHING. Please don't stop! *You're almost there!* You are more clear than ever about what you're doing, but it can also be the biggest fallout behind the scenes of what your life used to be like too! It is massive to hold both realities at the same time. Keep going. To have such big extremes play out behind the scenes is normal, and many go through it, but no one talks about it. Keep. Going. You can literally cry every single day for 18 months and wonder, 'WTF is wrong with me?' I am here to tell you—you are *healing*. There is a time and a place for connecting with your spirit guides, inner child healing, past life work, wound clearing, and all the yummy metaphysical things, and yet, the most powerful healing howling cries can take people off medications in a matter of months if they truly let themselves heal the deep grief their soul has been carrying for way too long. Society is trained to suppress grief. I am here to give you permission. It is okay to cry for 18 months and realise you are healing; there is nothing wrong with you.

3. Moving On. Now, don't mistake this for thinking that you'll be a happy chappy and everything will be rosy again. Well, it CAN be, but most of the time, at the start, it is a melancholy 'moving on'. Sometimes it can be waves of grief, but you're still moving on. You know it's over. You know the past is truly over now. You know that you can't go back. You know you've exhausted all your options, and they didn't work, and now, well, you're just...

here. In this space. And well, mostly alone, and well... now what? We grow accustomed to 'space'. Sometimes, we've been alone our whole lives, and now we're actually 'feeling' alone for the first time, and well, WTF do I do with that? It is like the unconscious living alone moves to consciously feeling alone, then shifts to a 'new space' you haven't felt before. Eventually, as time passes, you learn that magic is born in this space. That infinite possibilities, all scenarios, all realities, and everything you could do and desire are in this space, in this path of the unknown, that the Earth appears before your feet as you walk it, and you start to remember that this...

Is Who You Are.

You're a magical, amazing person who loves life and always has, and you've regained your spark for life, and you feel so much freedom, joy, and love again for life and yourself. Remember that you were born to do this. With or without them. With or without the person. With or without the support. With or without the career, the title, or whatever. You shouldn't even be thinking about that anymore because you're back doing your thing again, and well, thank FUCK for that.

But it is a journey.

A healing journey.

And it takes time.

And if you're not feeling the zest for life and deep self-love for yourself more than you've ever felt before again, you're still in one of the other stages, okay? It's coming. And that's okay.

Funny things happen when you come out the other side of such a journey.

You're stronger than ever before.

Your boundaries are like rosebushes of steel.

You're so savvy about bullshit—more than you ever were before.

Your Purpose is clearer than ever before.

And you just love life again. Ah. Relief!

And the Rose Bush Analogy? A beautiful blog that I wrote in July 2018:

The Rose Bush Analogy

So many in society are walking around with closed hearts, hunched shoulders, and sad minds.

And these closed hearts?

They have either a shield of armour protecting them, guards, concrete walls, or something similar.

Because, honey, most people don't know how to protect themselves from getting hurt again. (By the way, spiritual protection and protecting your energy are old-school these days! But that's another post!)

You see, the only thing that is real is LOVE. So when you close your Heart due to past pain from a relationship hurt, trauma, or otherwise, you do so to protect yourself from getting hurt again, right?

Well, it doesn't quite work like that.

You may think you are protecting yourself from getting hurt again, but what you are actually doing is shutting out the LOVE that is present right now!

Because all that is now is Love: someone gifting you something, someone saying you look good today, someone offering to carry your bag for you, or someone holding a door open. 'Oh, that never happens to me', doesn't it? Or are you just so closed that you don't notice it?

Life is abundant; life is NOW.

So if you have built concrete walls around your Heart, honey, you may feel isolated, alone, and sad most of the time, like you don't belong, are left out, and are very alone (oh, did I say that already?) Because the number one key to feeling alone is a closed Heart.

Think of the first person from a previous relationship in your past that comes to mind. This is where you need to start unravelling the hurt and pain instead of holding onto them.

Because it is only creating armour and concrete walls around you and your Heart, preventing any new Love from entering your life now. Is that what you really want? To be blocked from receiving Love NOW?

You may even feel disconnected, isolated, and alone, and you may be IN a relationship now. If this is the case, do the same. Where is the hurt coming from? That is the first thing that comes to mind. And it may be from your current relationship sitting there, and that is okay. Release the hurt.

Opening your Heart back up doesn't mean you won't get hurt again. You are human, and we have emotions as human beings.

But what it does now is make you feel connected, happy, and joyous again. (Oh, you've forgotten what that's like, haven't you?)

And what it feels like to be held, loved, and nurtured… and the all-important sex that we all secretly crave…

But what is most important about bringing your walls down is that you will be open to attracting and receiving them again! That's what you want, right?

'Yes, but I don't want to get hurt again!'

Of course, no one does.

The Rose Bush Analogy first came to me when I began teaching Lightfilled Yoga in 2012.

Instead of concrete walls, shields of armour, or completely closing down your precious Heart, replace those shields and those concrete walls with a Rose Bush.

The Roses beautifully open and RECEIVE the LOVE in the right now (because that is ALL that there is right now), and the thorns on the Rose Bush will catch any negativity that comes into your field, energy, or Heart. It will catch them like pieces of cotton, and the cotton threads get stuck on the thorns and eventually disintegrate just like cotton does.

Yet, the LOVE passes right on through...

So you are protected AND can open your Heart again, babe.

Because isn't that what you want?

To be loved?

What are you waiting for?

Replace Those Walls With Your Rose Bush.

There is a difference between spreading awareness and curiosity and fear-driven anger and rage at the government and others 'for what they are doing to us'.

And you know what?

This is the breakdown before the breakthrough of your Life Purpose.

You can't change the world and build better systems that support humanity when you are still operating under the old paradigms.

You're angry at the government for what 'they are doing to us' and 'ruling your life'. Yet, you sit there and happily receive government money and other benefits every fortnight and are throwing shit in their face for it, not making any changes in your own life, but getting up and doing the same fucking thing, complaining about the same fucking thing like what? *That* doesn't make any logical sense. For real. This? It is an old paradigm. You're complaining about shit but not doing anything to change it. This is #1: Awareness. #rantover Perhaps it is not you who is reading this, and I celebrate the way you've taken your power back. The ones who feel powerless on the inside and powerless in their own lives, combined with childhood pain and adult pain and hurt they have buried and not felt, are 99% of the time very angry, judgmental as all fuck, and usually quite negative and abusive people.

Living off-grid, hiding away in a cabin in the woods, is only wanting to stop burning out, trying to save the world, changing your own life, and running away from the pain you're about to face.

There's nothing wrong with going off-grid to live a sustainable farm life, but check in with the 'why', with the motivator behind your why. If you're doing it to get away from people and run away from pain, make sure you heal your deepest wounds and reassess if that is what you still want because, once that isolation from civilisation hits, you'll be wishing you'd be back to the convenience of civilisation quick smart, once you realise you have no choice but to face the pain of your past. You can't run away from it. Perhaps you need to go off-grid and away from everything without distractions and normal routines to be able to see what is really happening underneath. The true Healers are the ones who are not afraid to be in the thick of it when SHTF because they understand the power of trusting where they are called to be. If that is where they are meant to be, then that is where they are meant to be. Trust Your Intuition the entire way.

All of these fears arise when you have been working on yourself. When you have been healing and consistently doing personal development or manifestation work of some kind for a decent amount of time, it will come to a point where your deepest fears and traumas surface. They are coming to consciousness because they can no longer sit in your unconscious mind and energy field.

That was the whole point of you doing the manifestation and personal development work in the first place; however, most of the time, most people don't realise the immensity of the change that occurs in their reality to bring their dreams to life. That is the point of healing and making changes in the first place—changing something that is not working or has become unhealthy in their life and creating a better life *by* doing the personal development and healing work. Or simply because you want to.

The other part that no one speaks about is that increasing and strengthening your intuition in whichever way, shape, or form, whether through specific intuition classes, meditation or yoga practises, breath work, or ice baths, *will* bring the deeper unconscious traumas to the surface.

I see it time and time again: the ones who teach 'intuition only' 99% of the time do not know how to deal with the deep trauma that surfaces. They leave people in it, which can send them to mental illness, institutions, and addictions if they are not cared for properly when someone's deeper stuff is surfacing. Please, whatever you do, recommend them to someone who knows what to do with them. I have a database of trained Healers with this expertise for this very reason.

You'll be referred to time and time again if you admit your limitations and refer them to someone who knows how to deal with the deeper trauma, rather than saying they can't be healed or trying to do something outside of your jurisdiction. That is like a knee surgeon trying to do brain surgery. Yeah, you can imagine the implications and fallout from this. The spiritual industry needs to be regulated in the same way. Until that happens, work within your knowledge capacity or gain skills in what calls you to learn such techniques further.

It is okay not to want to work with deep trauma; it is definitely heavy work, especially if you have not healed yourself or know what you are doing. Just admit your limitations; otherwise, this industry gets a bad wrap, and people flick to Christianity (for example) and start calling us witches and the devil's work simply because deep trauma is surfacing that they don't know how to deal with it and sends them into unconscious judgmental, negative people because they simply do not have an understanding of what is happening to them when they have been so consistent with their persistent developmental work.

To become more psychic, you release and heal the deep traumas, which we can see as cloaks and backpacks of bricks, so they are 'not blocking your vision'. When you are shifting your life and healing from your past to create a better future, not a repeat version of subconscious creation, your deepest fears and traumas from childhood and past lives *will* surface. Change is the only constant, yet many also fear what it brings to their lives. We are creatures of habit, so change can be scary. Anything is scary until we get used to it. Learning to ride the waves and get through them is key.

The other important factor here is that when you have these immense fears of the world collapsing beneath your feet or the tsunami coming, it is also a literal past-life fear of when our Earth really did do that. You are not making stuff up or being crazy; you're remembering past lives in real-time. You only need to search 'mud flood' or explore 'Tartaria' to discover our Ancient past. I believe it is much bigger and more vast than just Tartaria, but it is a good place to start if it is new to you. They say that 'history' is actually 'his' story, training society in a way that keeps us unconscious. But as I always say,

You Can't Stop Consciousness Awakening.

What is important here is to clear the scar tissue layers from the relationships and the lifetime of childhood and adult experiences you have lived through that we have mentioned so that you are not ungrounded and on constant edge, living life in a state of fight or flight, making unconscious choices that send you further into the hole. Just because our Earth is due for another catalytic event, it could be another five centuries before the actual big change happens, and here you are, living like it will be tomorrow. No, honey, you're here to live life fully, in joy, not fear. It is the past traumas surfacing that will keep you living in fear with a cap and cloak on you. You are here to live with an open heart, enjoying all that life has to offer and experience. That is the point of being here.

Trust Your Intuition.

I don't like sending people down rabbit holes when I share things I have learnt or seen, but rabbit holes are sometimes how people wake up to truths but also get lost and attached to dogmas simply because they are trying to make sense of their reality in a world that doesn't make sense on top of a pile of unhealed trauma that they are subconsciously carrying and also can't make sense of. It is so important to trust your intuition when you are called to watch, read, or understand certain things. I love it when my students in my Trust Your Intuition to Become a Certified Intuitive Healer and Life Purpose Activator Course, absolutely get this.

If I watch or share something from something I watched, they won't force themselves to watch it just because I was talking about it and making sense of what I saw to share something I was understanding. A living example of this is in one of my classes. I was sharing something about a show I watched, and a student shared how she and her son watched a show (one that I don't resonate with or like), and they received the same message in a different show! It was a prime example of this.

Your Intuition Is Always Showing You.

In a way, only you understand. This is where I say, 'Ego desires, Soul desires—they are all the same'. This leads on from 'You are your intuition'. If my student was trying to force herself to watch something that resonated with me and not with her, and yet she forced herself just because it's something I got so much out of, she would be confused, irritated, distracted, frustrated, sink into depression, or even just conform. (Sound familiar?) Whereas she put her tools into practise, trusted her intuition instead, and received the exact same teachings from another source in a way she understood and what I also call 'learning through joy'—following your passion, your heart, your interests, what you love, not sitting there forcing yourself to do something or watch something you hate. Who does that?! Yet, the sad reality is that the latter is how society is trained—until they heal the mother, father, and God trauma bond wounds to take back their power, deeply trust themselves and what they love, and stay connected to their very powerful intuition.

It is common to start a project and then get distracted by ten other things while trying to complete project number one. I always say to my students, 'If halfway through Trust Your Intuition you're called to do four other things, trust the timing of it because it is leading you somewhere and activating certain skills that allow you to complete what you're here to do'. Other students will finish my Trust Your Intuition Course from start to finish without any 'distractions', and there is no right or wrong. I have frequently mentored several Inner Circle clients by trusting and expanding their skills through completing ten projects at once without thinking they are losing themselves, losing their lifestyle at the same time, or being distracted and not finishing what they started. It is so important to know that multi-tasking is a skill and a gift. Alongside the fact that most of the time, if one project weren't distracted by five others, you wouldn't have been able to finish project one.

How often do you clean your home (unless you have a cleaner, of course; however, let's just use the cleaning example for a moment) and find yourself doing ten other things you didn't plan to do in this current clean, but it all flowed and led into another and allowed new ideas or ways of being to enter into your reality? This is trusting the intuitive flow. This is who you are. This is your gift. Own it. There is always a time and a place to focus on one thing at a time, especially when you're close to the completion of a major project. However, you're not scattered or a mental case; you're deeply connected to the truth of who you are and what you're here for, creating new systems that match the natural intuitive flow to support humanity's ability to thrive.

Some people label distractions as sabotage, entities, or demons that are taking you off track. Entities, demons, and negative influences can distract you from your Purpose and show up when you are about to bust through to a new level. Don't let them!

Notice them, wave at them, smile at them, and tell them you're going to keep going. Stick your tongue out at them, ignore them, turn your back on them, and BUST that glass ceiling, precious Soul! I believe in you!

Yes, you can cut cords and clear demons and entities with meditations, and while sometimes these are definitely called for, the fastest way to shift them is just doing your damn purpose work! #simple! Entities, demons, or any negative influence are only a reflection of your deepest subconscious fears:

- That you're not good enough (but you are because you exist);
- That you don't know what you are doing (but you do because you wouldn't have the vision for your purpose for no reason; it's your inherent divine blueprint, and you do know how to do the thing if you would just block the world out and do the damn thing);
- That you do not believe that you have what it takes (but you do, because you wouldn't be reading this if you didn't, and God doesn't give you anything you can't handle, especially the Life Purpose that you said yes to, which is also why you are here!).

Demons, entities, and negative influences can also come when you are off track. If you're ignoring your intuition and not listening to your intuition about leaving a certain situation in your life, you become a beacon, or more like a rotting piece of meat that the flies are drawn to and don't leave alone until it is gone. They swarm on you and will drain your energy, make you sick, tired, and upset most of the time, and make you wonder if you're Martha or Arthur going crazy and around in circles while you continue to walk down a path that was over long ago.

To free yourself, you have to muster up the courage to follow your intuition from this moment forward, busting through that glass ceiling and allowing it to free you and your Soul to get your energy and life back by deciding and then acting upon your Soul's path. The fears that halt your Life Purpose are distractions, put simply: emotions that surface that are very uncomfortable to face and that have surfaced because *you have* been doing the work. I go into detail about demons, entities, and distractions in Trust Your Intuition to Become a Certified Intuitive Healer & Life Purpose Activator and also in the Throat Chakra Consciousness Course.

Red Flags to watch out for in yourself when you are continually being distracted from said feelings that are uncomfortable to face and are ruling your life, taking you away from your true Soul's Life Purpose:

- Attaching to dogmas and shoving them down everyone's throat.
- Blaming other people for your life circumstances (including the government).
- Too scared to leave situations that you *know* are unhealthy and toxic for you (of course, domestic violence relationships can be dangerous to leave, and you are advised to get specific help and planning with this).
- Just want the next meditation, plant ceremony, breath work session, light code, healer, or magic pill to sort out your problem/issue/wound/trigger.
- Complaining about situations but not doing anything about changing them.
- Stuck in a negative mindset and don't even realise it (sometimes people will say to you how negative you are, or you hear through the grapevine how draining you are to be around).
- Telling people you're going to commit suicide but not going ahead with it.
- Deep into addictions, even the 'It's just a little bit every night'.

While your Life Purpose involves in some way sharing your passions, interests, and what you are naturally good at and what you resonate with the world in some way, shape, or form, there is a differentiation between being deeply hurt and yelling it at the hilltops for what you stand for and shoving it down everyone's throat that they need to live this way because you are hurting underneath, and to face that is too painful, so it is better to bandage it up and tell everyone else how to live instead.

Simply live your truth and share your message in a powerful way by living it. You can still 'shout it at the rooftops', but the undertone will be different, more subtle, potent, and stable because you have healed your pain and reconnected to your truth. Your truth is being 'shouted' instead of the pain covering it.

It is common to teach your biggest pains in your current reality to get you through to your next level. There is no shame in this. However, it is definitely a healing process that can leave you lost for a little while as you recalibrate back to your truth instead of the pain leading the way. You will lose old clients, friends, and family along the way. Don't let this stop you. You are coming into a potent, more powerful way of living your life and activating your true, core Life Purpose. Grieve about it? Gosh, will there be! The ones who are meant to stay on your path will.

You may find that everyone falls away; this is also normal and not something many talk about. It is also a reason many don't fully lean into and follow their unique individual Life Purpose that isn't on the planet yet, because when you're bringing an entirely new perspective, systems, and creations to the world, no one will understand it but you. This takes an incredible amount of trust in oneself and just doing it without needing outside validation or worrying about what others think to make it happen. This can be hard when, in the beginning, most times, it is the ones closest to us that will tear us apart. Build it and do it anyway.

The Only Thing Stopping You Is You.

When you live by the Life Purpose Rules, you can literally make anything happen. Your biggest visions become your blueprints for unlocking and living your Life Purpose. You take the next step with what you have to make it happen now, no matter how long it takes, because you know your Purpose is here for Life, and you're here for your Purpose, and if that takes your whole Life, well, what on Earth else are you here for? People can be distracted for years by world stuff and even 'stay there' with it while others are out there creating solutions for it because they trust themselves enough to go against what normal society expects of them and to follow what is calling them inside, no matter what anyone thinks or what happens along the way. The difference between the ones who are making it happen and those who are not and are still complaining about x, y, and z is that the ones who look within are deep enough to heal the deepest, hardest trauma holding them back.

It is not even the person's fault that they are 'not looking at their traumas surfacing'. We know that the current society doesn't accept feelings and emotions, and you're crazy, or something is wrong with you if you cry. When I was mauled by two dogs and taken to the hospital for five days, I cried the entire time. I frequently had nurses come up to me and ask me in a roundabout way if I needed to speak to a professional or if there was something wrong with me without saying it. I couldn't believe it. I was crying to heal from what happened because, fuck me. I almost died from something I love, let alone how traumatic it was.

On one of the later hospital visits to get stitches out, I even saw a sign with a clown on it, saying that they have a clown come in to distract kids from their feelings on certain days so they don't cry while being treated. I wanted to tear down the sign. The system needs to be changed, and my purpose is to do just that. If people cannot express their emotions, how the fuck are they supposed to heal? Talking about feelings is different from feeling them. No pill heals feelings. It only suppresses it. Yes, I know to follow the money trail, etc. I know you know... but we also know there is another way, and that is what Ancient Blooded Healers are here for—to help people truly heal and come back to their true nature to live their true Life Purpose, not a shadow version of it.

There is a time and a place for medications and other modalities that help a person get through a certain time in their life when nothing else is working for them, and they haven't found the right healer that truly understands them yet. That isn't what I am talking about; it is about understanding how simply crying can heal so much, yet society shuns it as something wrong with your mental health. No. Tears heal. Tears serve a definite purpose in your body; otherwise, you wouldn't have them. They release the stress hormone cortisol from your brain—cry more!

It is not a person's fault that they choose not to heal at this time. That doesn't mean you need to continue to subject yourself to their negativity or abuse; definitely not. When you set boundaries with said person, you'll probably get a barrage of something from them. The systems, support structures, and true healing methods of trauma release—even the true understanding of trauma—are distorted in society.

Most of society thinks that trauma is some massive car accident, the death of a loved one, or a major event in someone's life, and yet, the smallest change in a person's day can create trauma. It's not a person's fault they choose not to heal at this time, but it also isn't your mission to wake them up to it. We all know that you cannot change someone, let alone heal someone! The person has to be ready for that themselves. True change only happens when you're ready and willing to heal yourself. The teacher appears when the student is ready. Your only mission is to be the teacher when the student is ready.

When you know this, live this, and focus on your mission, you will be frowned upon for not 'attending the rallies to fight for our freedom'. The true creatives on this planet just won't be drawn to such events. They know where their power lies. The ones who are on the fence and not grounded in their mission or unclear about what they are to do regarding their Life Purpose will feel guilty for not going and cave to the crowd pressure and go. Sure, they might be intuitively guided, but if you don't want to go and are guided to focus on your Purpose Driven Mission and Solution, trust yourself over any crowd guilt tripping you into such. It may as well be your family pulling you down for staying true to your Life Purpose!

If any of this has struck a chord with you, been hard to read, triggered you, or resonated with you, it is time to heal. It is time to stop focusing on what 'they' are doing and deeply come into your own heart, which is full of pain. It is time to face this pain, to truly feel the core of this pain, so you can get back in alignment with your true Soul's path before all those things happened to you that pulled you off the path, made you close your heart, and turned out your light. The biggest distraction is that you don't see this truth and continue ranting, raving, and screaming while no one listens and thinks you're a raving negative lunatic! I don't want that for you! I know you can heal, step into your true power, open your heart again, and be so deeply grounded in your truth that people pay attention to you, listen to you, start asking you questions, and want to work with you without you chasing them down! I know this is possible for you, and it is my mission to help you rise into the true

Ancient Blooded Healer That You Are.

Chapter 8

Stepping Out Into the World As An Ancient Blooded Healer

When you step out into the world, proclaiming your gift in some way, shape, or form, if not straight away, then not too long after, there will be some kind of backlash. Some people around you will surprise you and support you for a time, and then when you reach a certain level of success, they will either celebrate with you or disappear from your life. I pray that you have the strength to continue your Life Purpose work no matter who walks away from you. I pray that you gather a solid network of support from like-minded Souls living their Life Purpose Passion around you to continue with your Purpose work, no matter what comes your way.

But who am I kidding? You're an

Ancient Blooded Healer.

Of course, you're going to continue, even if life comes along and knocks you down for six and some. You get back up every single time. Because that is who you are. You know what you have to do on this earth, even if it isn't clear to you, but at the same time, there is no way you cannot walk this path; there is no way you cannot do your thing. This is what you were born for; this is what you are here for; it is in your BLOOD.

Whether it is people, things, events, or situations, it will seem that every time you step up and out in some way, shape, or form, life will come bounding your way to see if you are *really* going to continue on this new path, this powerful path that you are taking to take back your power and change your life. It will be like, all of a sudden, life gets ridiculously busy; people will come out of the woodwork for whatever reason, rhyme, shape, or form, needing whatever from you.

Good and bad things will happen—to test you, if you will (not that I like using the word test!), to see if you are *really* going to do this. It will be the most crucial time to put those boundary things in place you've heard about but haven't yet implemented; it will be the time to feel the guilt of taking the time to do what you're being guided to do. Feel the guilt and do it anyway. Over time, that guilt will become less and less because you'll feel amazing for doing what your Soul is guiding you to do. You'll become stronger because your Soul is stepping into the driver's seat instead of just your human self trying to do it all on your own. It takes two to tango: your Soul and your Human Self (some people call that the Ego Self; another word I don't like—Ego! It is who your Human Self is; there is nothing wrong with your Human Self—your Ego!).

Usually, life will be amazing, but then it will reach a certain point where all these things seem to fall apart. Physically, things can break down in your house, car, electronics, and relationships—things seem to go wrong all of a sudden. Finances need a deep overhaul and lots of attention. It's okay. Don't let them stop you! It can be a huge drama, but you can decide that shit is happening, life is happening, and it is just something to deal with. Perspective Shift. Change your mind and approach it differently, and it will work out differently.

The only reason it will be a 'huge drama' and hard to handle is if we still have huge trauma from our past we haven't dealt with because it will be sure to surface during this time, making everything harder. Sure, we can look into the metaphysical reason behind everything, but sometimes, to not go cray-cray amongst so much change, we can allow things to be as they are and just deal with things. Life is happening, and we are just dealing with it, and sometimes this takes all our energy and focus for a time. This is normal; be okay with it.

Things are coming up to be dealt with, whether it is your emotions and past traumas or physical things that need tending to. It is all perfect and meant to be. It is cleaning out and preparing your clean slate for the new chapter of your life to start. Remember, to build a new house, first the old one needs to be knocked down or torn apart. To change the oil in your car, the mechanic needs to empty the old one and change the filter (and whatever else they do). To clean out the cupboards, everything that is no longer required needs to be pulled out before new stuff is put in there. It is normal for things to fall apart and seem like everything is against you continuing on this path. The number of times I have said to clients, 'If I had let technical issues stop me at the beginning of my online business, I wouldn't be where I am today'. Sometimes I have sat on the phone for 3–4 hours or more trying to figure out whatever technical thing was going wrong on my website or otherwise. Just six weeks after starting my online business, my computer told me it was too old to use the new program I needed to run my business after I had 90% of it set up already. I couldn't believe it at the time.

Trust me! It was a miracle that I had the money come to me for a new computer at this time. It was weeks of figuring it out, praying, taking action, stomping my feet, and screaming at the sky, 'If I am truly meant to do this work, help me, FFS!' Not that I would've given up anyway, but it took literally weeks of fucking around to make this happen.

If I had 'taken it as a sign that I wasn't meant to do it', I wouldn't be here writing this book for you. There are some things we aren't meant to do (sure, we could hire a website builder), but that isn't the point of my sharing that. I was a single mum, and I *had* to find a way to make it work on my own. I literally didn't have the funds for anything I needed back then, let alone a new computer or website builder! If I had let the technical issues and constant frustrations of learning an online business technical aspects alongside learning the business side of things and staying in my intuitive self at the same time weigh me down, I simply would not be where I am today. It was a big learning curve in the masculine structure, physical, technical computer stuff, discipline, and boundaries of my time compared to my creative feminine intuitive flow; it was so distinct for me to switch from one to the other, let alone having everything online instead of the physical. It was the biggest learning experience I went through, apart from the technical stuff, and I see why many Ancient Blooded Healers don't go the whole way because of it. If I took every little hiccup, block, stuck feeling, and the busy situation in life as a sign I wasn't meant to do this, if I had taken every little interruption while writing this book as a sign I wasn't meant to write it, well, you know what I am going to say.

Life happens. It is what you do about it that counts. Bad things happen. It takes ages to heal from traumatic events, and it takes ages to heal from not even traumatic events! The reality is that life happens, and we have to deal with it, sort it out, and find new and creative ways of living our lives. Of course, things have meaning, and it can help with understanding, healing, and forward movement to understand what certain signs and metaphysics mean. I train healers in this for a reason! Yet, we don't have to understand everything to heal it, and we can sort things out without looking too far into it. Don't let yourself get lost down the healing rabbit holes. Heal, but stay on Purpose.

Your trauma does not define you. Your trauma is only waking you up to a deeper part of yourself that wants to be expressed, to become whole again, and to show you deep down who you really are—under the trauma. The transformation and truth of who you are. You can become bitter or better. Which do you choose? Easier said than done, yes. However, walking *through* healing your traumas will allow you to become better. I hope this book has given you hope that you can heal, become better, move on, and truly be free to live your true Life Purpose—the one you have after the trauma has healed. There is a whole new you, a transformed you, and a whole new world awaiting you after this—are you ready to discover it? Who you truly are as an

Ancient Blooded Healer

Be kind and compassionate. If you can't be this, it simply means you need to cry, you need to heal, and you need to howl. You are at a timeline convergence point of a huge breakthrough point, and you should let yourself be supported during this time as you heal. Get support from the true Healers who have walked this path and know how to hold space at this level. You are not crazy. You are a powerful Healer who feels *everything*. You just have to heal and hone your skills, precious ones. That is all.

When you feel lost, let yourself be. When you don't know which direction to take, take none. You will know when that intuitive clarity drops in because you will feel it in your bones. You know what that 'OMG THIS IS IT!' feeling feels like, and away you go doing your thing again. When you're at a recalibration point and feeling lost, wait until that *OMG YES* feeling comes in. Until then, allow the recalibration to happen.

If you're tired, sleep more.

If you're not making money, sell more.

If you're not happy in your relationship, get fit and healthy, heal your inner traumas, check timeline convergence points, change yourself, and then reassess. After these changes, clarity will come as to whether it really is the relationship, career choice, or other major life decision you need to make or whether you need to tend to yourself.

Subtle shifts layered up constantly over time create dramatic changes. Don't underestimate the power of consistency in anything you choose to do. Remember the Life Purpose Rules:

Whatever You Do, Do It Consistently.

You can heal, get back on track, and remember who you are. You can do it moment by moment, day by day, little by little, and then it *becomes you*, and one day you'll wake up and it is all you do, day in and day out, and look back at the incredible life you have created. When you've been creating an amazing life and then things fall apart, remember that you're recalibrating. One day it won't seem like things fall apart; it doesn't even enter your mind. You just deal with stuff with barely any emotion attached to it and realise how far you've come. When you 'hit a wall' about something not working in your life when you know you're meant to do this but it is like all these things crept up on you, it is the *belief inside of you* that you can't do it, that's it. Shifting this internal belief to 'I CAN do it' can be the flick of the switch that creates magic in your life. You can do all the external factors and have been working for years on something when you almost 'forgot' about this potent power switch of belief in yourself, which changes the entire game. There are switches at every level, so when you feel this, remember to flick the switch of self-belief.

I Can Do This!

It isn't about how much more you need to do. It isn't about how much more you need to create. It isn't about how much more you need to strive to make things happen. You're past those stages! The thing that will tip you over into making it happen at whatever level you are at is your *belief in yourself that you can*. Usually, we hit this point when we've lost everything and everyone, but we are pushing through because this is our Life Purpose, and we wouldn't be doing anything else anyway. Giving up isn't an option. As many times as we've thought about walking away and have done so in our minds a zillion times before, we just can't. It is here—when everyone has lost hope in us—that this magic switch is you believing in yourself. There is only so much a mentor, friend, partner, or someone else can believe in you before the belief switch in you changes the game, makes everything happen for you, and makes you the most successful person on the planet in the field of your gifts—it is YOU believing in you. It is more than just 'I CAN DO IT' as a mantra in your head. This is a full-body, fully embodied 'THIS IS WHO I FUCKING AM'.

When the dogs mauled me and I came out of trying to get my life back on track and recover from what had happened and all the trauma from deep down that was surfacing from beyond the dog attack, I had my computer screen savers come up with: REMEMBER WHO THE FUCK YOU ARE. It took me a while, but I got there. And came back with a vengeance!

Sometimes we need to kick our own butt into gear. Well, every time we do! It is only we who can do that! You know this! You can listen to all the self-help audiobooks, go to every seminar, take all the courses, and work with high-level mentors, but at the end of the day, none of that is any good if you aren't going to take the leap of faith and just do the damn thing that you know you're meant to do. There is a season for learning and healing. Then there is a season for putting into practise all that you have learnt. Sure, there are always layers at every level 100%. But there is a definite shift when you are learning and healing all of this and then getting the nudge to start putting it into practise in the capacity that the Universe is sending you—either clients, ideas, or both. Act on them. Start before you are ready and figure it out as you go. Remember The Life Purpose Rules:

It Doesn't Need To Be Perfect, But You Do Need To Show Up.

The only reason you won't is because it isn't on the planet yet; you're too scared to dive so deep into your subconscious to heal the scar layers and uncover what is waiting for you beyond the healing. I hope that this book has given you the courage to realise that there is nothing to be scared of. Feelings aren't scary; society's beliefs and ingrained dogmas are what is scary. Your past-life fears are what makes it scary. Your belief in yourself (or lack of it!) is what makes it scary. Hanging around the wrong people who continue to put you down and disempower you is what makes it scary.

Your Soul knows what to do, how to do it, and how to create all the resources you need to get it done. All you need to do is build that inner connection to your Soul, make it strong, and turn up to it every day. You will be shown the way, but you have to turn up to be shown the way. Remember, *The Life Purpose Rules*:

The Messages Will Come Through <u>When</u> You Are Doing It.

The Next Step Will Be Shown To You <u>When</u> You Are Doing The Current Step.

When you get stuck and bogged down, return to the basics. Take some time out. Get back to nature. Spend two hours minimum in nature, and repeat until you feel better. Give yourself permission to step back for as long as it takes to reconnect with yourself and find your feet and your path to get you back on Purpose. There will be something you have done in the past that you can draw on to give you strength and inspiration, and you will know you can do it again. To remind you of your power and to remind you that you CAN. Sometimes we need to take a new turn, start something new, and take a new path. Sometimes it is drawing on what we have done in the past that has worked and doing that again!

The things that are powerful are very simple! We try to make them complex and complicate them, but they are so simple, and we forget that. Stop making it so damn hard. You've already been through enough. Draw on what you've done in the past that worked and do it again. And if you haven't done something, draw on others. Meaning that if they have done it, so can you!

Remember, it is your belief in yourself that is all that is required to make magic happen when all seems lost—to be able to do the things you love and the things you're good at, block out all the naysayers, and do what your heart is calling you to do.

Charge what you want to charge.

Say what you really want to say.

Dress how you really want to dress.

Be who you really want to be.

Live how you really want to live.

All in an instant.

Just. Like. That.

Take the aligned actions every single day, or what you're intuitively guided to do, of course, but if something is not working, believe in yourself and do not give up!

Keep going until. Then keep going some more. It will seem hard when you begin, but it becomes who you are. Always remember this. There is always a mess when new realities are born. You become a Walking Transformer, shifting things as you go. Remember, you're an

Ancient Blooded Healer

And you're

Born For This.

Don't underestimate the time it takes to build the life you love.

Don't underestimate the time it takes to grieve and heal to create a new slate for creating the life you love. But you are here for the Life part of your Purpose, right?

I thought so.

Don't get stuck; get back to basics.

Don't give up; take breaks instead.

Reality breaks and reality checks stop us from continuing down a path that isn't aligned. Be okay with taking breaks from what you are doing, especially if it is causing you frustration, so you can step back and wait for the 'OMFG YES!' Remember? You will know if you still need to do it (like sort technical stuff out or hire someone to help so you can continue on your path) or if you're meant to do something entirely different. Whether you're meant to leave the relationship draining your Soul and that you've been trying to make work but just can't no matter what you do. You will know. Your Soul knows. Be okay with Reality Breaks to reassess and let your Soul speak.

You have your life ahead of you. Your Purpose is meant for you, is waiting for you, and is here for you. But you have to be here for it too. Remember,

Life Purpose Rules:

Do What You Can, With What You Have.

Whatever You Do, Do It Consistently.

It Doesn't Need To Be Perfect, But You Do Need To Show Up.

The Messages Will Come Through <u>When</u> You Are Doing It.

The Next Step Will Be Shown To You <u>When</u> You Are Doing The Current Step.

Chapter 9
Final Words

People have called me a pseudo-spiritualist who has no grounding in reality. I say that I am ahead of my time. If you are to be a leader in this world, if you are to stand up for what you believe in, if you are to live the life you really want to live, I guarantee you will have pushback from someone or a group of people in this world. If you are to truly follow your heart, as the cliche says, you must learn and train yourself not to concern yourself with what others think of you; otherwise, you won't do it. Of course, at times, it will rock you to your core, and you'll be shocked, cry, howl, and not believe what's going on. Then eventually, you *will* continue. You *will* pick yourself up and continue on. I promise you. I also deeply believe in you. If I can do it, so can you.

The other reason you won't do it and stay shrunken and small and continue to dim your light not to upset anyone is that, at some point, you have lost the love and acceptance of someone close to you or that you look up to and have not healed from this yet. There is still time to heal, to take your power back, and to do what you were born to do. That is why you are here, with this book in your hands, because this is your sign, your permission slip, and your pathway to healing so you can live the life you were born to live, birth the mission you came here to contribute to Awakening the Consciousness of Humanity, and enjoy it at the same time, no matter how dark the path has been that took you down and re-birthed you to shine your light, joy, and very tapped-in consciousness on this planet that you are on.

You are a beacon of hope, a way shower of light, the one everyone turns to when they are in their darkest time or don't even realise why they are sharing with you what they are. What you are here to do in this world is not on the planet yet. You are not here to fit in but to stand out—another cliché. What this really means is that you are here to create systems and structures on the planet that are not here yet. This is why you've never felt like you fit in, belong, or resonate with what or how anyone else does it the way they do it—because you are simply not meant to.

You will outgrow people.

You will outgrow relationships.

You will go off and, probably for a time, turn against everything that once was good for you and then shout it at people because you've just moved away from it.

You're healing.

You're on a journey.

Do not judge yourself, and catch yourself when you judge others.

You are a powerful Healer here to contribute to the evolution of humanity's consciousness in some way, shape, or form. Not everyone is like us, even though we think so, and then we wonder why everyone looks at us like we are weird!

You're a Leader, dear Ancient Blooded Healer.

It is time for you to step up and claim this; that is all.

There are many pathways and modalities for healing. Try what your intuition is calling you to, and when you find what works, trust it with all your heart and follow it all the way home. If nothing works for you, or if it does for a time and then something else calls you from what you've learnt, and something else is trying to bust out of you, it is because it is! You're here to create a new one. Trust your unique Life Purpose that is busting out of you, guiding you to heal your past so you can clearly hear, understand, and have the courage to live what you were born here to do.

You can heal.

You can live again.

You can smile again.

You can find your heart and your life again.

You're not here for no reason.

You're an

Ancient Blooded Healer.

And you're

You're One of A Kind.

We are only just beginning.

Where to From Here?

My Ancient Blooded Healer Activation Meditation is a beautiful activation of your Ancient Blooded Healer Self. Through a 26-minute journey of beautiful ceremony, your Ancient Blooded Healer is reclaimed and activated. This meditation can be used for:

1. Release anyone and anything holding you back from your authentic, truest self.
2. Activating Your Ancient Blooded Healer Lineage through Lumeria, Atlantis, and Avalon
3. Activating Your Sacred Earth Lineage
4. Healing Blood & Thyroid Related Issues in your physical body
5. Reclaim your truth from abusers, people who have betrayed you, hurt you, or made you feel like they have torn parts of your Soul away or stolen your Magic. No, this isn't about blame, but reality; when traumatic situations happen, there are pieces that also happen. You get to reclaim them now.

Check the website for the Ancient Blooded Healer Audio Meditation here www.realityawareness.com/audio-meditations or scan the QR Code here:

Trust Your Intuition to Become a Certified Healer & Life Purpose Activator is my internationally recognised Certification Course that takes you through your healing journey to heal you and step into becoming one of the greatest Healers on the planet because you've lived this, walked through it, healed from it, and stepped into the wisdom that you are.

Whether or not you want to become Certified, you have lifetime access to this course and can work at your own pace. Doors open at varying times; check the website www.realityawareness.com for all the details.

You can follow Hannah here:

Instagram: https://www.instagram.com/realityawareness/

Facebook: https://www.facebook.com/realityawareness

Reality Awareness Healers

If you would like to be mentored by myself or if you would like to be intuitively matched with one of our trained Healers registered with the Certified Reality Awareness Healers, please email us at: support@realityawareness.com.

We Would Love Your Support!

If this book has helped you, shifted you, changed your life, and healed you, we would be so grateful if you would please leave us a review on Amazon. Thank you so much!

www.ingramcontent.com/pod-product-compliance
Lightning Source LLC
Chambersburg PA
CBHW070252010526
44107CB00056B/2431